Thyme after Thyme

The secrets of consistent good cooking

RICHARD SMITH & ADRIAN COOLING

To my newly-born son William Edwin for opening a new chapter in life. To my amazing wife Victoria for her support and inspiration. To my mother Pauline for her advice and guidance. All my love.

Richard Smith

To all my friends and family and to all those I have worked with – particularly Max and Susan Fischer and, not least, Richard and Victoria Smith.

Adrian Cooling

Out thanks to the following; Adrian Walsh of Food and Fine Wine, Ecclesall Road, Sheffield, for the wine recommendations; David Mellor for the cutlery; Nick Munro for the jelly mould in our raspberry jelly recipe; to Thyme and Thyme Cafe staff for their help and hard work – in particular Simon Wild, Tim Vincent, Ian Robley, Ryan Hodson, Jack Baker, Mike Thompson and Hayley Conroy; to Hannah Edwards, for her patience while daddy was tied to the computer screen for days on end; and to various individuals who kept up an endless supply of coffee that fuelled the team's efforts.

PHOTOGRAPHY: **Peter Goulding**
EDITORS: **Martin Edwards and Matthew Chambers**

Published by:
Thyme,
32-34 Sandygate Road,
Sheffield S10 5RY

All material herein is the copyright of the publisher
and is not to be reproduced without prior written permission

CONTENTS

INTRODUCTION
7

ABOUT THYME
8

HOW TO USE THIS BOOK
10

CHAPTER 1
Café Culture
11

CHAPTER 2
Classics
35

CHAPTER 3
A world of flavours
61

CHAPTER 4
Desserts
81

CHAPTER 5
Extra Thyme
Basics and side dishes
105

CHAPTER 6
Wine and food: a brief guide
115

INDEX TO RECIPES
121

INTRODUCTION

Just about anyone, on a good day, can produce something in the kitchen they can be proud of. The trick lies in doing it every time.

Consistency is everything in the restaurant kitchen. Anything less than the best, every time, is unacceptable. The customer isn't interested if a chef's had an off-day. He just doesn't come back again.

To cook a dish well takes more than luck. It takes good preparation, a method that works and a bit of know-how as well. That's what we aim to pass on in this book.

Thyme after Thyme is not aimed at the professional chef. It is aimed at ordinary people who love cooking and would like to do it better. We've deliberately set out to demystify food. So you won't find here any impressive-sounding but incomprehensible chef-speak. Our intention is to present a tempting and varied selection of recipes you will enjoy at home, in an easy-to-follow format. But we've added a special extra ingredient – in the shape of a few tips we've gleaned over decades working in the restaurant business. Our message is that creating good food is fun, rewarding, and within the range of anyone.

Enjoy the book.

Richard Smith   **Adrian Cooling**

8   THYME AFTER THYME

ABOUT THYME

In 1994, Richard and Victoria Smith saw their ambition transformed into reality. After years working abroad, cooking at internationally-famous venues and for some of the world's most celebrated businesspeople, they returned to Sheffield to open their own restaurant. But it didn't stop there and soon the couple set their sights on another project. Smiths gave way in 2001 to a restaurant on an altogether grander scale and with a formidable team behind it in the kitchen. Thyme was born.

Even at their most optimistic, they could not have imagined what would happen next. Thyme wowed both diners and critics alike. Writers from all the major national newspapers sought it out, proclaiming it had put Sheffield on the dining-out map. Within a few months, the awards followed; including no fewer than four Restaurant of the Year accolades from magazines and newspapers. Less than three years later, Thyme Café opened under the stewardship of Richard's long-time friend and colleague Adrian Cooling. The Café was the less-formal sister to Thyme, although both still carry a banner for the same cause – innovative, unfussy food cooked to the highest standard. This book contains a selection of the dishes that have featured on both menus over the years.

HOW TO USE THIS BOOK

"The greatest mistake you can make
in life is to be continually fearing
you will make one".

Elbert Hubbard (1856-1915)

Enjoy cooking? Then this book's for you. We've produced it with the enthusiastic home cook in mind, and with the deliberate aim of de-mystifying good food. With even the most basic skills, you will be easily able to produce any dish in this book.

- At the end of each recipe, we've drawn on decades of collective professional experience to produce a short section of tips and techniques to help you get the best from the dish. Put those principles into practice, and you will indeed get consistently good results.

- Some dishes call for ingredients (such as sauces and dressings) that require separate preparation. You'll find these in the chapter entitled Extra Thyme, under the heading 'Basics'.

- Also in that chapter is a special section on simple accompaniments or side dishes. Find them listed, with methods, in the other half of the Extra Thyme section.

- With our eye on something to accompany your chosen dish, we've included a detailed section on wine styles. For quick reference, each dish has its own recommended wine style (or styles) represented by a number. Simply refer to the wine section and you'll find more detail about that style, including some examples of it.

- In addition to suggesting suitable styles, our wine correspondent has also included his own personal choice to enjoy with each dish.

CHAPTER 1
CAFÉ CULTURE

CAFÉ CULTURE

ITALIAN SAUSAGES
with polenta mash & tomato sauce

This is sausage and mash as you've never seen it before. It's a good example of a classic northern Italian style that's really in vogue right now. But for me, it's reminiscent of one of my stranger culinary challenges. I was called on to cook this very dish for a houseful of hungry students not so long ago when a colour magazine decided to put me on the spot. It was a little strange cooking in the cramped kitchen of their house, but the dish was a huge hit. The fact that the magazine supplied a few free bottles of the essential accompaniment, namely some Italian red wine, no doubt helped. **AC**

INGREDIENTS
3 Italian sausages per person (approx 80g each)

Tomato sauce
½ chopped onion (approx 120g)
2 crushed cloves garlic
1 x 400g can chopped tomatoes
    (canned cherry tomatoes are ideal)
80g olive oil
Pinch salt
Ground black pepper
Pinch of sugar

Polenta mash
100g double cream
200g instant polenta
800ml boiling water
30g butter
75g grated parmesan
10 g chopped parsley
100g chopped onion
3 cloves crushed garlic
Pinch of salt

METHOD
To make the tomato sauce
1. Gently sweat the onion in the olive oil without colouring. Add the chopped garlic and cook out for a minute.
2. Add the canned tomatoes, salt, pepper and sugar. cook gently over moderate heat for about 10 minutes. check seasoning. the sauce should then be ready to serve.

Sausages and polenta mash
1. Sweat onion and garlic in olive oil.
2. Add the boiling water.
3. Stir in the polenta and cook for 1 minute.
4. Stir in the butter, grated parmesan, seasoning, cream and herbs.
5. The mixture should be like mashed potato in consistency. be careful – hot polenta can boil volcanically when heated. Serve immediately .
6. Meanwhile, fry the sausages gently in olive oil until nicely browned. Finish cooking in a baking tray in a moderate oven for about 10 minutes.

CHEF'S TIPS

Italian cookery is all about good quality but fairly basic foods combining to great effect. And it's the basics that make or break this dish. You can buy Italian sausages from the supermarket but the best ones are to be found in Italian Delis. They're not hard to spot – look for the big, fat peppery variety, tied up with string and occasionally flavoured with fennel seed.

Now a word about tomatoes. Don't be afraid to use the tinned variety. But beware. Use a poor quality brand and the dish will suffer. In fact, there's every possibility it could end up as an insipid, flavourless shadow of the genuine article. An Italian chef I once worked with swore there was a conspiracy at work in the tomato industry. The Italians, he told me in all sincerity, export the poorer quality tinned tomatoes to nations which know no better. The best they reserve for themselves. Whatever the truth of that dark theory, buy the best quality you can lays hands on – the extra cost will pay dividends in the finished article.

Our third basic ingredient is polenta, now very trendy and a feature on the menus of many expensive restaurants. It's a classic case of rag to riches, because polenta was, and in the eyes of some still is, a peasant food. Don't let that put you off. Try it the traditional way, finished with parmesan and parsley. Or, for a bit of variety, serve it with basil mash instead. **RS**

RECOMMENDED WINES
5
6
Chianti Classico Leonardo

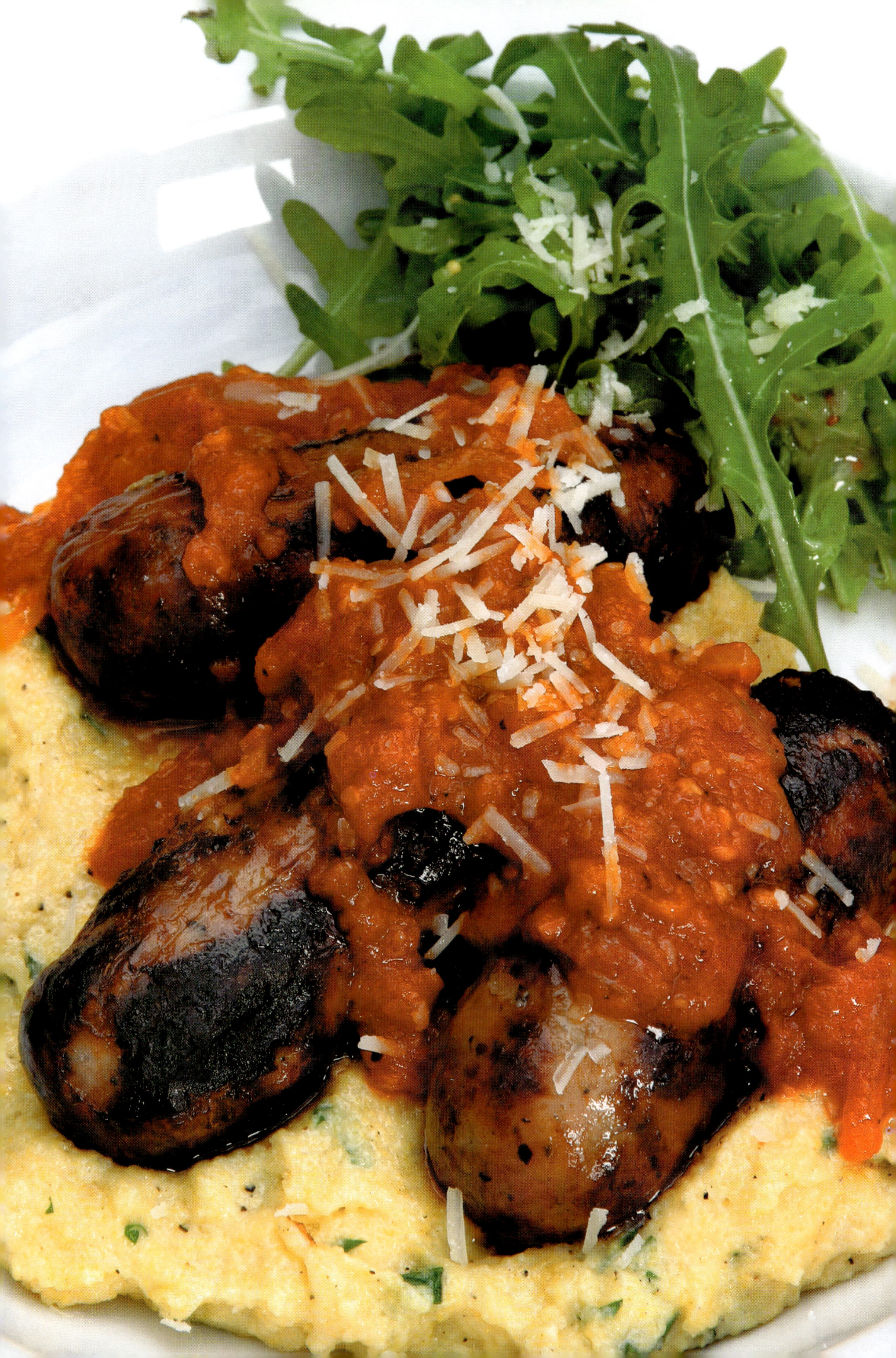

CAFÉ CULTURE

SMOKED HADDOCK GRATIN

Café culture may be a relatively modern phenomenon, but this is a dish from the old school. Leeks always go well with smoked haddock, and here the crispness of the leeks is excellent when set against the smoky flavour of the haddock. The contrast between these two textures and flavours is the crux of the dish, but if you'd prefer to use an alternative to leek, go for potatoes or penne pasta. I believe this to be just about perfect as a lunch dish, and here's the proof: as I write, I'm preparing for an event where it will be served as lunch to over 200 people. That's the beauty of this gratin – it's easy to prepare in advance, and can simply be stuck in the oven when needed. **AC**

INGREDIENTS

900g natural smoked haddock fillet, skinned and boned
1 litre milk
500g thinly sliced washed leeks
200g butter
110g plain flour
Salt
Freshly-ground black pepper
250g grated mature cheddar
50g grated parmesan

METHOD

1 Pre-heat oven to 180°c.
2 Place the smoked haddock fillets in a roasting tray, cover with milk, and season with black pepper. Cover with tin foil and bake in the oven for about 10 minutes, or until the haddock is just cooked. Pour off the milk and reserve it for later. Keep the haddock to one side.
3 In a saucepan, heat up 100g of the butter, stir in the shredded leeks and sweat down until the leeks are cooked, but are still crispy and green in colour. Season with salt and pepper. Place in the bottom of the serving dish and top with the flaked smoked haddock.
4 Melt the remaining butter in a saucepan, and when it starts to bubble add the flour. Stir in and cook out for around 3-4 minutes, until a sandy texture is achieved – this is known as a roux.
5 Slowly add the milk to the roux, a little at a time, and stir continuously until a good Bechamel sauce is achieved. Should you wish, you can now add a little cream to give a luxurious finish to the sauce.
6 Stir in the parmesan and cheddar, reserving some for topping the dish.
7 Pour the finished sauce over the haddock, top with the grated cheese, and bake for 10-12 minutes. serve .

TO SERVE

Serve with a rocket and French bean salad and warm, buttered Jersey royals.

CHEF'S TIPS

The luminous yellow-dyed smoked haddock that's ubiquitous in supermarkets may look weird and wonderful, but it certainly has little impact in terms of taste. Stay away from those vacuum packs and you should be all night, as most decent supermarkets will have a fish counter selling the un-dyed variety. Failing that, it's easy to get hold of at a good fishmonger's. As with all seafood, the all-important thing to bear in mind is that overcooking will ruin the fish. Leave it in the oven for five minutes over its allotted time and all that's left is a tough, inedible, rubbery substance. As you reach the stage of pouring over the sauce, the haddock should still be translucent; remember, it has to be baked all over again. **RS**

RECOMMENDED WINES

5 3

Beaujolais Cru

THYME AFTER THYME

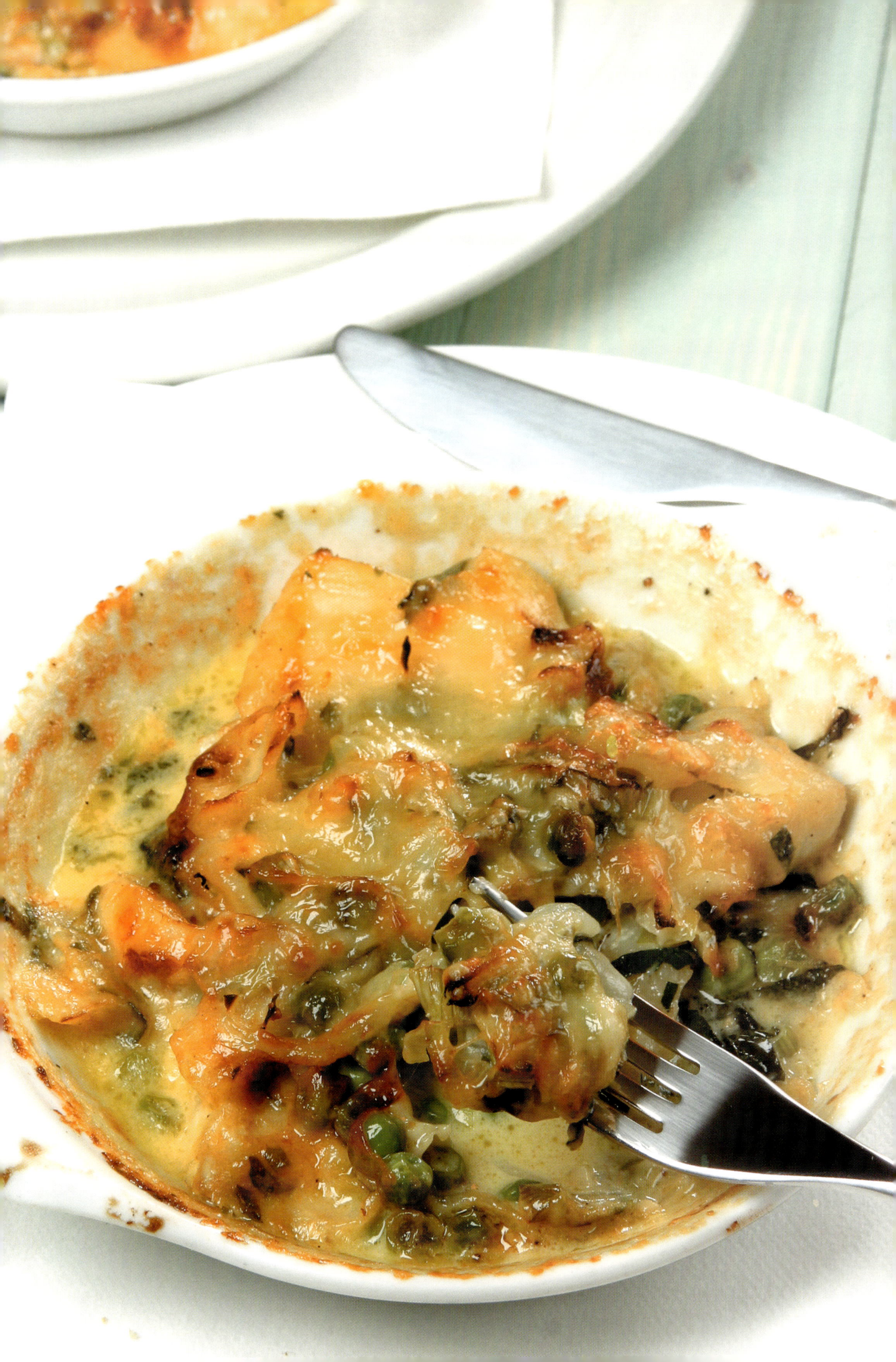

CAFÉ CULTURE

SHELL-ON PRAWNS
with dipping sauces

Tapas is massive at the moment, and everywhere you look new Spanish-themed eateries seem to be springing up. There's absolutely nothing wrong with that, as top-quality tapas combines a variety of flavours with a sense of the communal fun that food should be all about. This is a really fun dish, as people actually get involved in creating their own food, by tearing the prawns and experimentally dipping them into the sauces. Get a few friends round, pump out a salsa theme through the stereo, and watch as everyone reaches over each other to pick out the best-looking prawns. **RS**

INGREDIENTS
9 shell-on prawns per person
15ml chilli oil (see Extra Thyme)
Grated zest of ½ lemon
Juice of ½ lemon
Salt and pepper

METHOD
1. Toss the prawns in a bowl with all of the ingredients (you can also use olive oil as an alternative to chilli oil).
2. Place the prawns in tumblers and top with a wedge of lemon and a sprig of flat parsley.
3. Serve the dipping sauces in small tapas dishes.
4. Use the Vietnamese dipping sauce and cucumber and coriander raita sauce (see Extra Thyme). These two dips complement each other really well, as the Vietnamese dip is quite hot and fiery, while the cucumber is cool and refreshing.

CHEF'S TIPS
I always like to use opposing elements in my cooking. Contrasting hot with cold can be really interesting, and it's something that works really well here. The spiciness of the chilli oil and the Vietnamese sauce contrast beautifully with the cool raita, and choosing for yourself in what quantities you want to experience the different flavours is part of the fun. If it all sounds a bit modern for your tastes, or those of your guests, you can always timewarp back to the seventies and include Marie Rose sauce as well. **AC**

RECOMMENDED WINES
2
5
Eden Valley Petaluma Riesling

16   THYME AFTER THYME

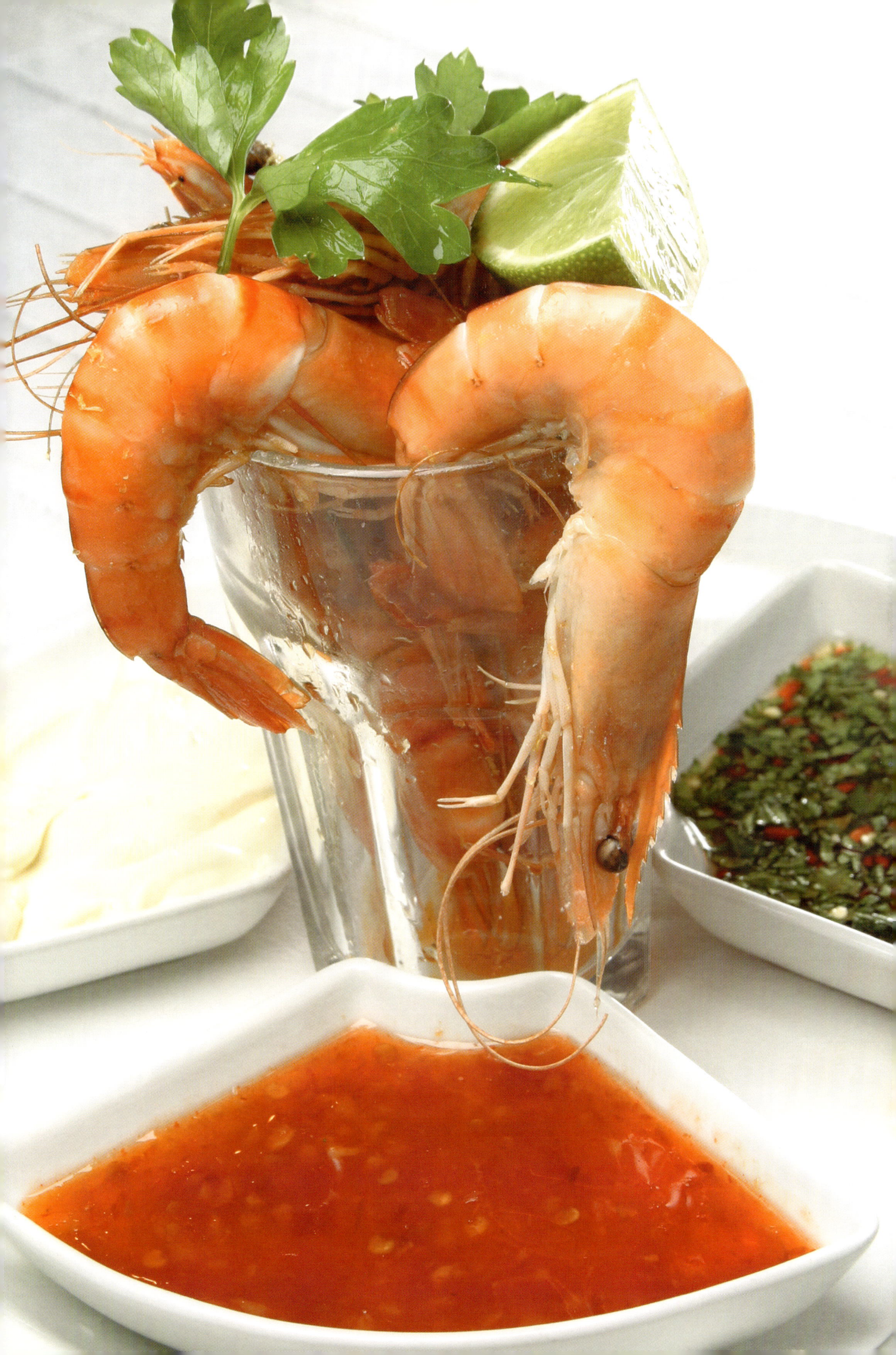

CAFÉ CULTURE

PASTA GENOVESE

What, pasta with potatoes? Carbohydrate with carbohydrate? Did they not teach us anything at catering college? Well, yes, since you mention it. This is one of those dishes that shouldn't work, but it does. Look at it this way; the Italians have been eating this superb regional dish for ages so it must be good. As a nation, they have a reputation for admiring and creating ostentatious things – Ferraris, expensive clothes and of course sunglasses, which are worn at all times and in all weather conditions. But there is one matter upon which they can never stand accused of being flash, and that is in their cooking.

They are the masters at not over-complicating good basic food. Not for them the French passion for elaboration – turn a French chef loose and before you know it you'll be confronting enough mousses to run the length of the channel tunnel. *Mon dieu!* But if you must be a little fancy and want to produce a dish to really impress the guests, try serving this with a seared fillet of salmon on top. The two work really well together. **AC**

INGREDIENTS

600g baby new potatoes
500g trofie dried pasta
400g french beans
250g pesto
Freshly grated parmesan to taste
Salt
Pepper

METHOD

1. Cook the baby new potatoes in boiling salted water until just cooked.
2. Slice into 1cm rounds.
3. Cook the pasta in plenty of boiling salted water.
4. When just cooked (about 10 mins) strain and mix in with the potatoes.
5. Cook the french beans in plenty of boiling salted water for 5 minutes until the beans are cooked, nicely green but still crisp.
6. Drain and mix with the pasta.
7. Add the pesto and toss all the ingredients together.
8. Season with salt and pepper. Split evenly between 4 large pasta bowls.
9. Sprinkle generously with freshly-grated parmesan.

CHEF'S TIPS

A word about pasta. And no, don't throw it at the wall to check if it's done. There are better ways to establish that than by pelting the décor with the main course.
Your pasta will carry on cooking for a short while after it is taken from the heat and before it reaches the table. So check it a minute before the stated cooking time has elapsed. It should be slightly, and we stress slightly, on the firm side. At that point, turn off the heat and drain it.

There are some cooks who feel bad about using dried pasta, believing it's the inferior twin to fresh. Don't. It isn't. Fresh pasta is fine for tortellini and ravioli but otherwise choose a good quality packet version and the result will be fine. **RS**

RECOMMENDED WINES

Soave Classico

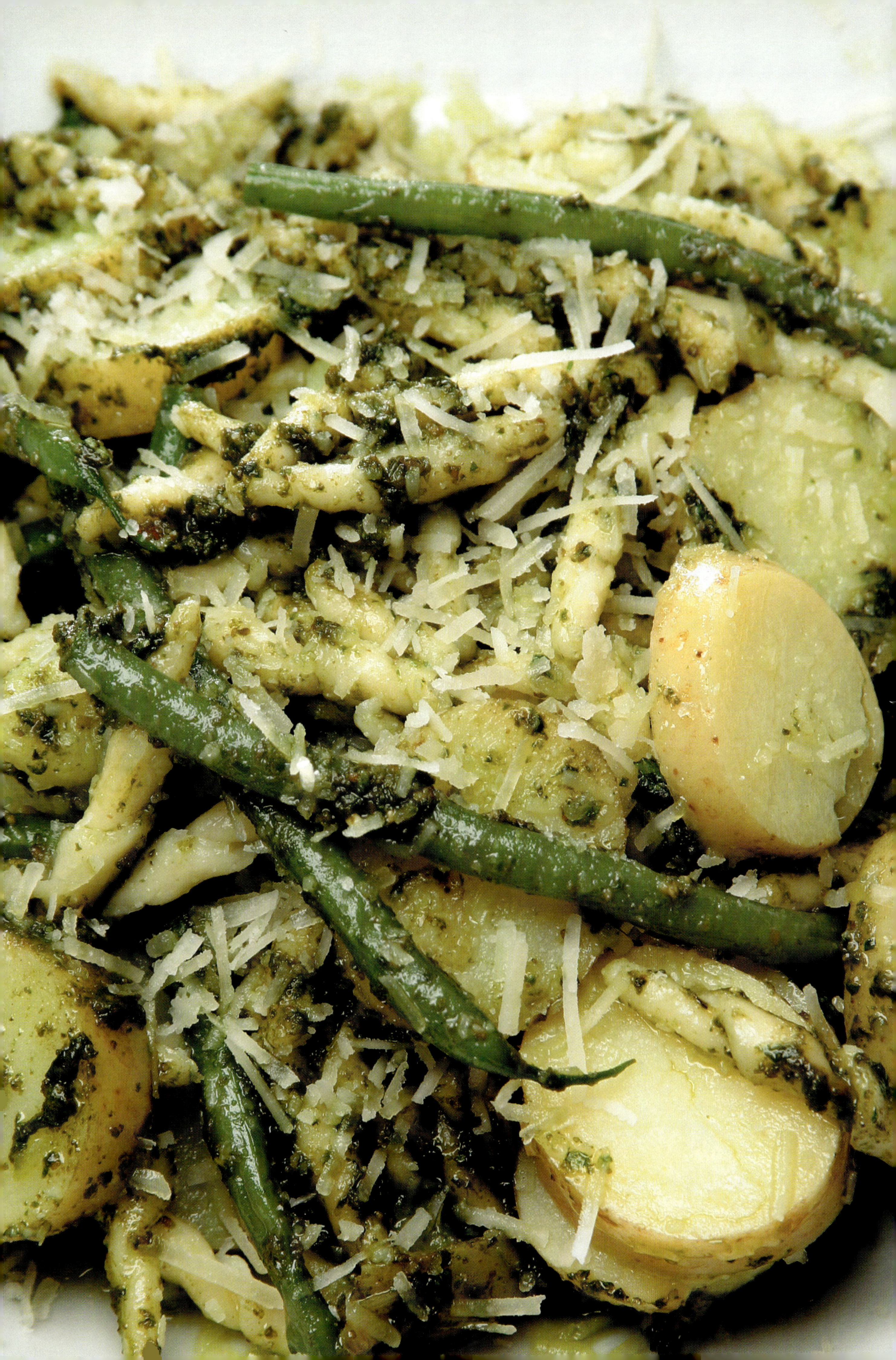

CAFÉ CULTURE

THYME CAFÉ CHEESEBURGER

It may not exactly have the best of reputations in serious food circles, but look down on the cheeseburger at your peril. Some chefs may question why it appears in a cookbook, but I love doing things like this. I'm not the only one, either – believe it or not, it's the best-selling dish in the Café! Thankfully, this version bears little relation to the awful mass-produced variety, save for its name. The burgers you chew on in the high street are so often full of fat, or rusk; by contrast, ours is full of pure meat, with the sort of good seasoning that makes all the difference. Popularising food amongst young people can only be a good thing, and for me it's the ideal dish with which to settle down in front of the television with a few beers. **AC**

INGREDIENTS

120g diced onion
3 garlic cloves
1kg best quality minced beef
1 chopped red chilli
50g tomato ketchup
30g brown sauce
15g Henderson's Relish
Small bunch of flat parsley, chopped
Salt and pepper

METHOD

1. Pre-heat oven to 200°c.
2. Sweat the onion and garlic in a little oil until soft, without colouring.
3. In a large bowl mix together the beef, onions and garlic mix, chilli, tomato ketchup, brown sauce, Henderson's Relish, chopped parsley, salt and pepper.
4. Form into rounds and flatten down with the palm of your hand (they should weigh around 250g each).
5. Fry the burgers in a large frying pan, with a little oil.
6. When browned on each side, place the pan in the oven for about 15 minutes, until the burgers are cooked through.
7. Top with the slice of cheddar, and melt for a minute under the grill.

TO SERVE

4 crusty bread rolls
Garlic mayonnaise
Plum tomatoes, sliced
Gherkins, sliced (2 long slices per serving)
Mature cheddar cheese (1 x 140 g slice per serving)
Small dressed gem lettuce (2 leaves per serving)
Red onion, sliced
Café ketchup (see Extra Thyme)
Bucket of chunky chips (see Extra Thyme)

ASSEMBLY

Cut the bread rolls in half, and spread generously with garlic mayonnaise. Place th burger on the bottom half. On the top half, place the sliced tomatoes, dressed leaves, sliced gherkins and sliced red onions. Serve open, with a bucket of chips and Café ketchup.

CHEF'S TIPS

As I've already pointed out, the seasonings are very important here. In fact, they are the making or the breaking of the burger. It's always good to get Henderson's Relish, that old favourite of Sheffield dining tables, involved, The chilli meanwhile gives the burger that extra lift that you will seldom encounter in a 'happy meal'. Also, make sure to use the best quality minced beef you can find. Much of it is full of fat and water, and will disappointingly reduce right down in size when you cook it. Opt for the lean stuff instead. **RS**

RECOMMENDED WINES

7

Cono Sur Pinot Noir

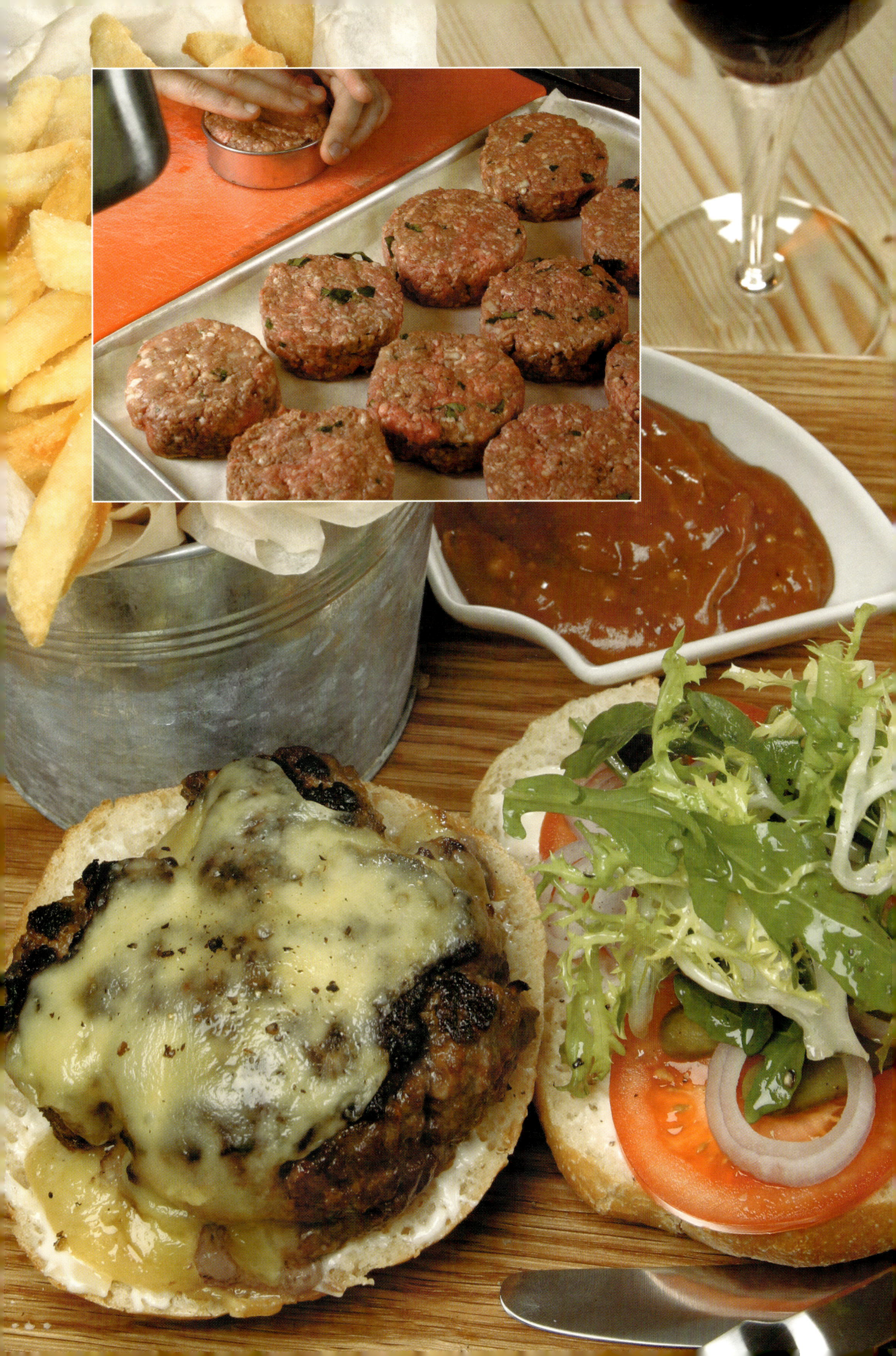

CAFÉ CULTURE

CHICKEN BREAST
with Mozzarella and parma ham

The idea of wrapping one meat in another is nothing new. As well as adding a second flavour to a dish, the technique has the effect of holding it in shape. However, the Parma ham brings a contemporary twist here, and the remaining ingredients continue the Italian theme. **AC**

INGREDIENTS

4 Chicken breasts
8 slices parma ham
2 buffalo mozzarella
Salt
Pepper
1 batch of tomato sauce (see Italian sausages recipe)
2 aubergines
1 medium chopped onion
2 crushed cloves garlic
8–10 cooked new potatoes
2 tbsp olive oil
2 courgettes
½ batch batter (see fish & chips recipe)
2 tbsp pesto (see Extra Thyme)

Tomato sauce
(see Extra Thyme)

Aubergine crushed potatoes
(see Extra Thyme)

Battered courgettes
(see Extra Thyme)

METHOD

Chicken

1. Cut 4 large squares of kitchen foil. Place 2 slices of parma ham side by side on top of foil.
2. Cut down the chicken breasts lengthways – just enough so that you can fold them out ready for filling (see photos opposite) and season.
3. Spread with ½ tbsp of pesto.
4. Cut the buffalo mozzarella in half and place on top of the chicken breast.
5. Fold the chicken breast over so the mozzarella is completely encased.
6. Put the chicken breast at the bottom of the parma ham and roll over so it is completely and neatly covered in parma ham.
7. Now roll in the foil then twist each end of the foil so it is tightly wrapped – this ensures a nice shape to the finished dish.
8. Place the chicken breasts in the fridge until 20 minutes before required.
9. Transfer them to a tray in a preheated oven at 200°C and cook for 15 minutes then remove from the oven and leave to rest for a further 5 minutes.

TO SERVE

1. Divide the aubergine crushed potatoes between the plates.
2. Cut the rested chicken breasts in half lengthways and sit on top of each other to reveal the pesto and mozzarella.
3. Sit the battered courgettes at the side and spoon around the tomato sauce. If you like you can drizzle with a little pesto, sprinkle the courgettes with grated parmesan and put a deep fried basil leaf into the aubergine crushed potatoes.
The dish works perfectly well without these but it does give it a restaurant style finish.

CHEF'S TIPS

No chef worth his salt ever underestimates the cooking skills of his mum. For whatever grand creations he might turn out in the professional kitchen, don't forget she was, almost without exception, master of that most difficult meal of all – the roast dinner. The co-ordination required to cook one of these would have an air traffic controller complaining of stress. Get it wrong and some soggy, overdone veg are on their way in for an emergency landing; one error of timing and the starter's on a collision course with the Yorkshire pudding. At any one time five or six items are in a holding pattern, awaiting the call to descend to the table.

This dish places slightly less onerous demands on the cook. Do your preparation, cook the potatoes in advance (the day before if you like) and life's suddenly easier. Likewise, have your chicken ready rolled in the fridge. But whatever you do, prepare the battered courgettes last of all, as otherwise they go soggy. Last of all, you'll need a good sharp knife to prepare the chicken. Sheffield-made, of course. **RS**

RECOMMENDED WINES

Montepulciano d'Abruzzo

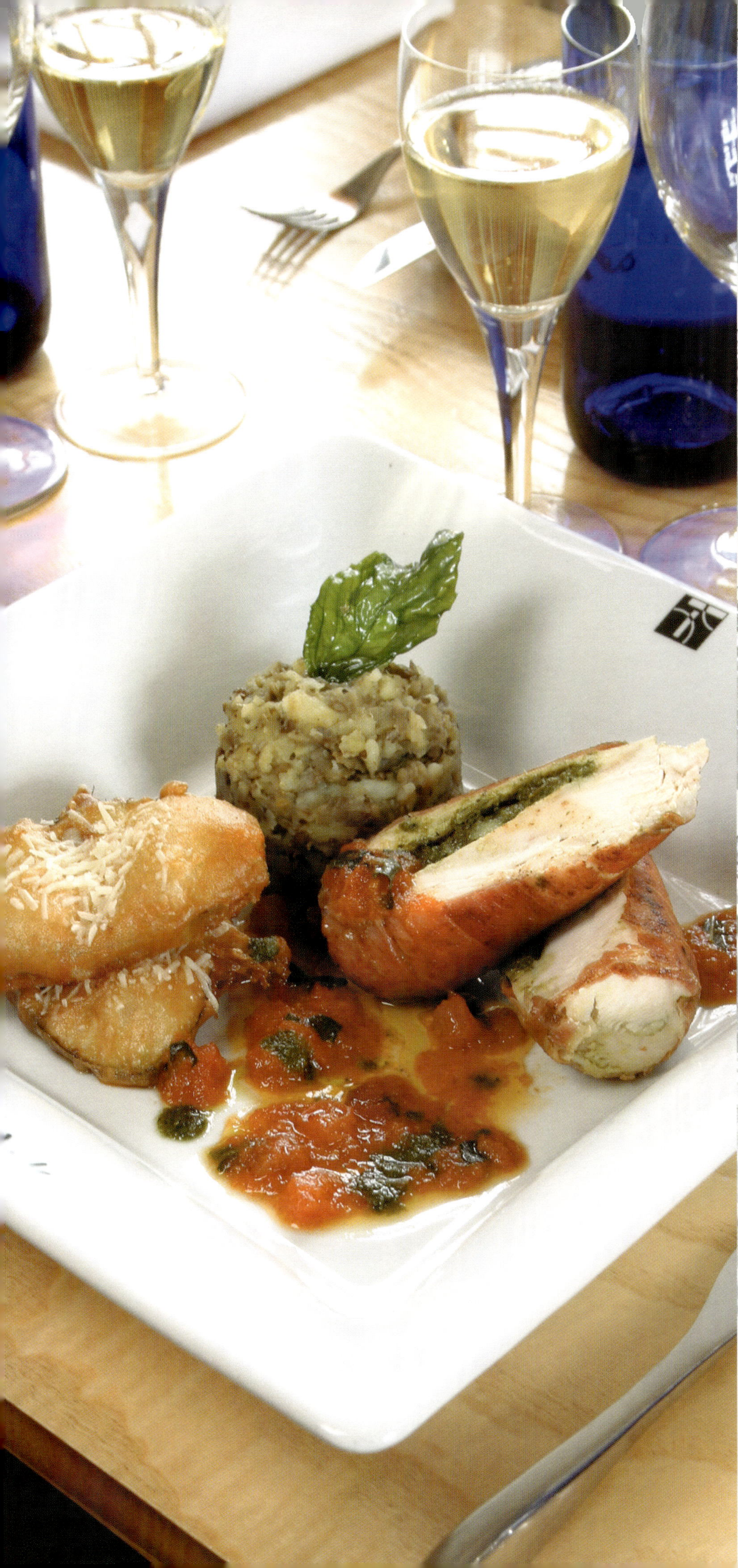

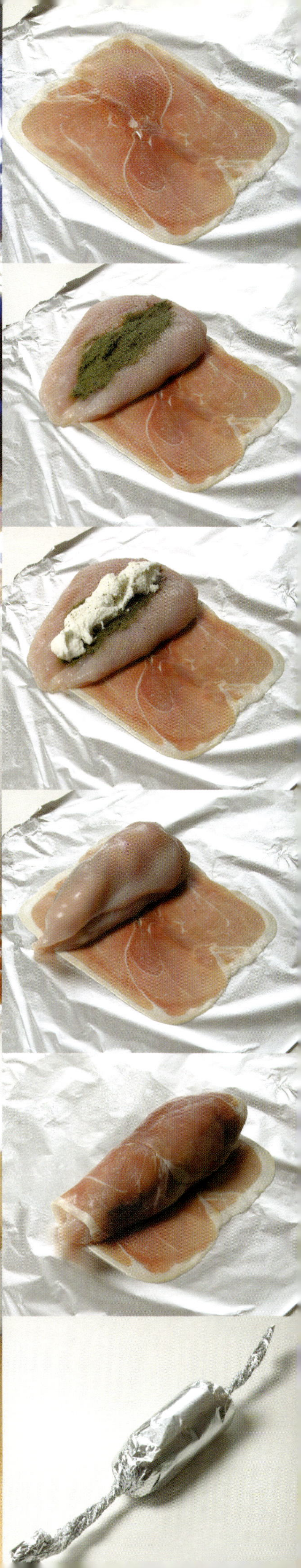

CAFÉ CULTURE

RED PEPPER RISOTTO

Most dishes owe their inspiration to something seen or sampled somewhere else. That's just the way of the restaurant business. This one came about by happy accident. So was it a sudden flash of genius, a divine spark from some remote corner of the imagination that brought it into being? Actually, no. It was the fact that one day we had a surfeit of red peppers in the café's vegetable store and we had to think of something to do with them. As is so often the case, we ended up creating the menu around what he had to hand.

The outcome was a dish with unmistakeable impact, thanks to its colour. It tastes even better than it looks and it's inexpensive – look at it as an alternative to *risotto alla Milanese*, with its saffron and even, from time to time, gold leaf in Italy's posher restaurants. **AC**

INGREDIENTS

Red pepper stock
50g olive oil
200g sliced onion
20g garlic
4 large chopped red peppers (440g)
1 litre vegetable stock

Risotto
75g butter
2 chopped cloves garlic
150g diced onion (1 medium onion)
400g risotto rice (arborio)
Red pepper stock
60g grated parmesan
100 ml white wine
Pinch salt
Freshly ground black pepper

METHOD

For the stock
1. Sweat onion and garlic in olive oil for roughly 4 minutes without colouring
2. Add chopped red peppers and cook for a few minutes. Ensure the peppers do not brown.
3. Add vegetable stock, bring to boil and reduce to simmer for 8–10 minutes.
4. Puree in blender. It doesn't matter if it isn't completely smooth – this gives a good texture to the risotto

For the risotto
1. Sweat onion and garlic in butter without colouring.
2. Add rice and stir until nicely coated with butter.
3. Stir in wine and cook until evaporated.
4. Add red pepper stock a ladle at a time and continue stirring constantly until the risotto is cooked. This will take about 20 mins
5. To finish the dish, stir in the grated parmesan and adjust the seasoning. spoon into bowls. top with dressed wild rocket and crumbled feta cheese.

TO SERVE

Dressed wild rocket (approx 20–25g per person)
Crumbled feta (approx 40g each)

CHEF'S TIPS

First and foremost, make sure you use the right variety of rice. Arborio is easy to find at most supermarkets, which makes it all the harder to fathom why one Italian restaurant I tried recently decided to serve up long grain instead. Then the reason hit me. It was boil-in-the-bag stuff they could have ready in a few minutes. All it then needed was a ladle full of sauce and Roberto's your uncle.

Whatever else that may be, and the word abomination springs to mind, it is not risotto. A proper risotto takes time to cook. It also requires your almost constant attention. Be foolhardy enough to pursue a distraction even for a fleeting moment, dare to give your stirring hand a momentary rest and your risotto will show you who's boss by catching on the bottom of the pan. So treat it like some exotic Italian beauty - make it believe you have eyes for it alone (at least for 20 minutes) and you will be rewarded.

After cooking, the dish should have a creamy consistency, though it's really a matter of taste – I actually prefer mine a little looser. As long as the rice is cooked, it doesn't matter.

The butter and parmesan at the end add a luxurious touch. **RS**

RECOMMENDED WINES

Pinot Grigio Sauvignon Blanc

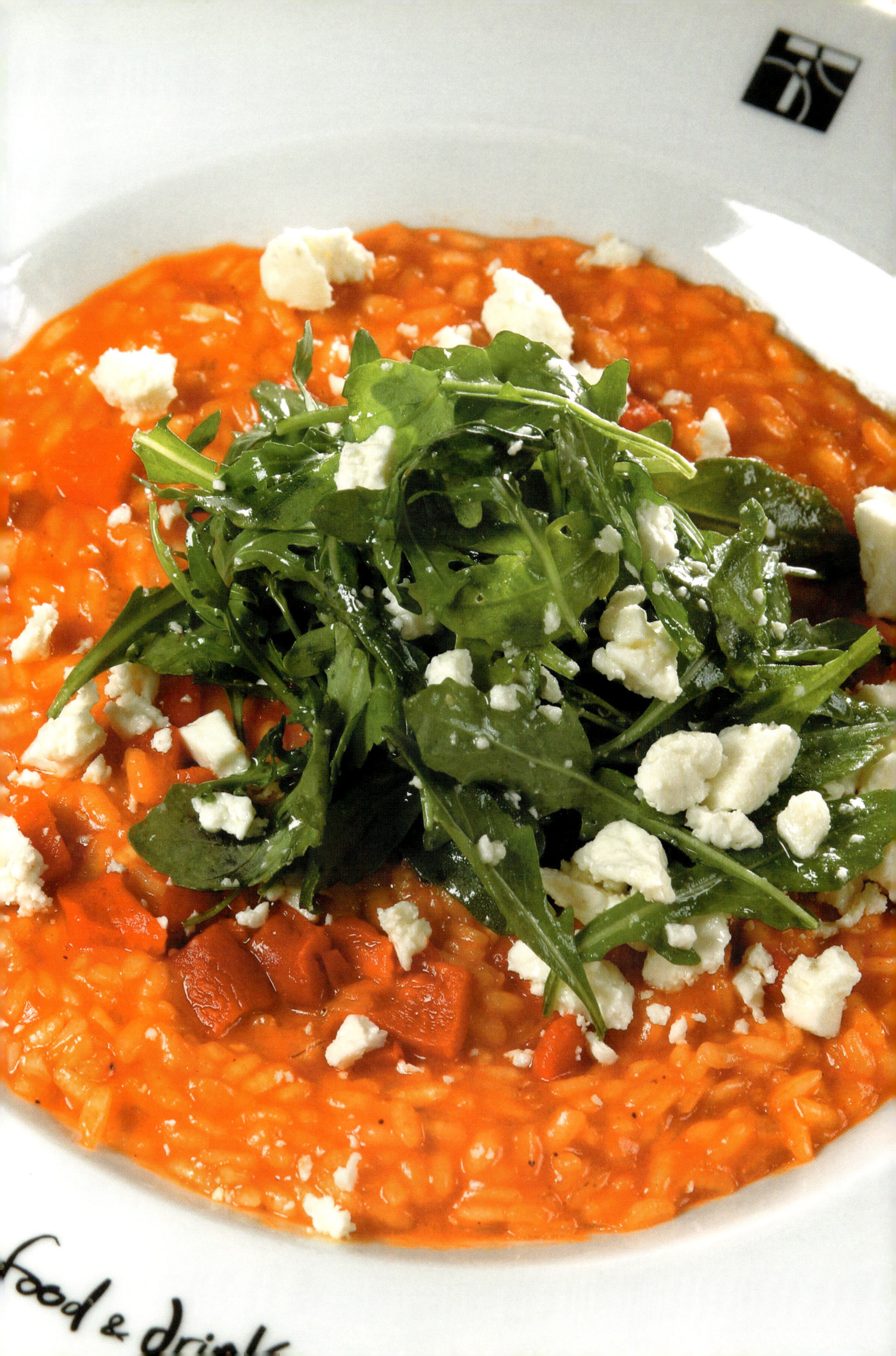
food &

CAFÉ CULTURE

SEARED TUNA
with mango–jalapeno salsa

If I was a marketing man instead of a chef, I suppose I'd be calling this a good example of Pacific Rim cuisine. But its origins can actually be traced to a corporate office block somewhere in rainswept middle England, rather than some exotic tropical island. It was there I found myself working on a project aimed at encouraging people to eat more fruit by using it in cooking. This was one of the recipes we came up with. The mango and tuna turned out to be a superb partnership, the fruit balancing out the competing flavours and the crispness of the onion. Whether you're sampling this in Hawaii or Halifax, I guarantee you'll enjoy the combination. **AC**

INGREDIENTS

4 fresh tuna steaks (200–250g each)
2 ripe mangoes
1 fresh red chilli
1 red onion, thinly sliced
100g extra virgin olive oil
2 cloves garlic, crushed
40g jalapeno peppers, finely chopped
25g fresh coriander, chopped
Juice of 1 lime

METHOD

1 Chop the mango into cubes, then add the red onion, red chilli, garlic, olive oil, jalapeno and coriander. Mix together with the lime juice.
2 Season the tuna steaks with salt and pepper.
3 Heat a frying pan until hot but not smoking.
4 Using only a little olive oil, fry the tuna until nicely browned (around 4 mins on each side). The tuna should still be rare on the inside.
5 Place the tuna on a plate, top with plenty of mango salsa, sweet potato and dressed rocket.
6 Serve immediately.

TO SERVE

Chargrilled sweet potatoes (see Extra Thyme)
Dressed rocket

CHEF'S TIPS

Tuna is one of those marvellous natural ingredients that are, sadly, so often spoiled by the way they are cooked. The key word here is 'seared', and that's exactly what you should aim to do. The first hint is not to use too large an amount of oil, otherwise it fries the fish. You need just enough to prevent the steak sticking. Put a small amount of oil on your index finger and smear the tuna with it just before it goes in the pan. That's all it needs.

Secondly, don't get the pan too hot – the steaks should be sizzling, not smoking. And finally, whatever you do, don't cook it for too long. You can only appreciate the true qualities of good tuna by keeping it a little pink in the middle. **RS**

RECOMMENDED WINES

8   3

Riesling Spatlese

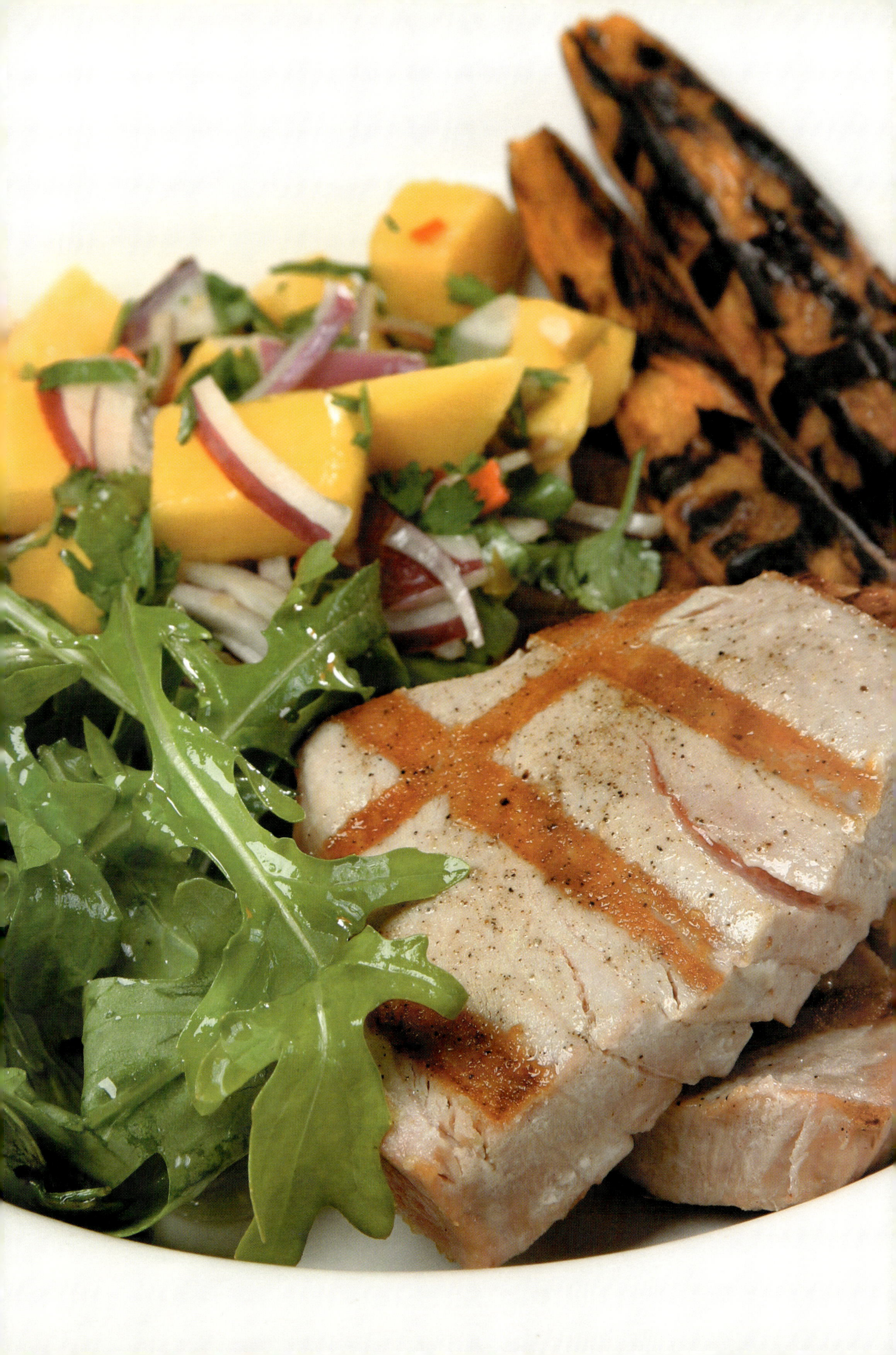

CAFÉ CULTURE

SPICY PORTUGESE PORK
and white bean stew

I'd love to be able to boast that I first discovered this dish at one of those undiscovered waterside restaurants, hidden away in a little village on the Algarve. But the truth of the matter is, I don't actually remember where I came across the idea. It certainly wasn't the result of a gastronomic tour of obscure Iberian eateries, though. In fact, I'm pretty sure some of its roots lay in a project I once did, in connection with gastropub dishes. We were looking at interesting ways of using cheap cuts of meat and one of my colleagues on the project, Sacha Ferrier, came up with the Portugese theme at a brainstorming session. Ideally the pork should contain a spicy tinge, but not one that's powerful enough to overpower the smokiness of the tender meat. The chorizo gives you a blast of heat right at the end, and the beans are good, filling fare. **AC**

INGREDIENTS

1 boneless side belly pork, skin removed
250g pancetta, chopped
1½ large onions, sliced
3 carrots, sliced
6 large garlic cloves, crushed
450g chorizo sausage, coarsely chopped
30g smoked paprika
50g tomato purée
2 x 400g tins of chopped tomatoes
2 red chillis, finely diced
4 litres chicken stock
Salt and freshly ground black pepper
250ml white wine
2 red peppers, sliced
2 yellow peppers, sliced
700g canned cannellini beans
1 large bunch coriander, chopped

METHOD

1. Dice the belly pork into chunky cubes, season, and seal in a hot frying pan.
2. In a large casserole pan, sweat the pancetta in olive oil. Add the sliced onions and carrots, and sweat down for around 5 minutes.
3. Add the garlic, chilli salt, pepper, smoked paprika and chorizo. Cook out without colouring for about 5 minutes, so that all the flavours are released.
4. Add the pork back to the pan, add the wine and cook out for a couple of minutes.
5. Pour over the stock, bring to the boil and reduce to a simmer. Cook gently for around 2½–3 hours, until the pork is very tender.
6. During the last hour of cooking, add the chopped peppers. Drain and rinse the cannellini beans and add them to the stew. Cook for 1 minute.
7. Serve in a terracotta pot with plenty of chopped coriander, and crusty or chargrilled bread.

TO SERVE
Plenty of crusty white bread.

CHEF'S TIPS

A relaxed demeanour is a must here. There are a lot of ingredients to deal with, and going about things in a mad rush is only likely to result in a lot of stress and an inferio end product. Prepare everything well in advance to ease the pressure, and really take your time. Cook it slowly, allowing time for the flavours to develop. You really won't need anything more than some good, rustic bread to accompany the dish, chargrilled if you so wish. **RS**

RECOMMENDED WINES

5   6

Journeys End Grenache/Cotes du Rhone

THYME AFTER THYME

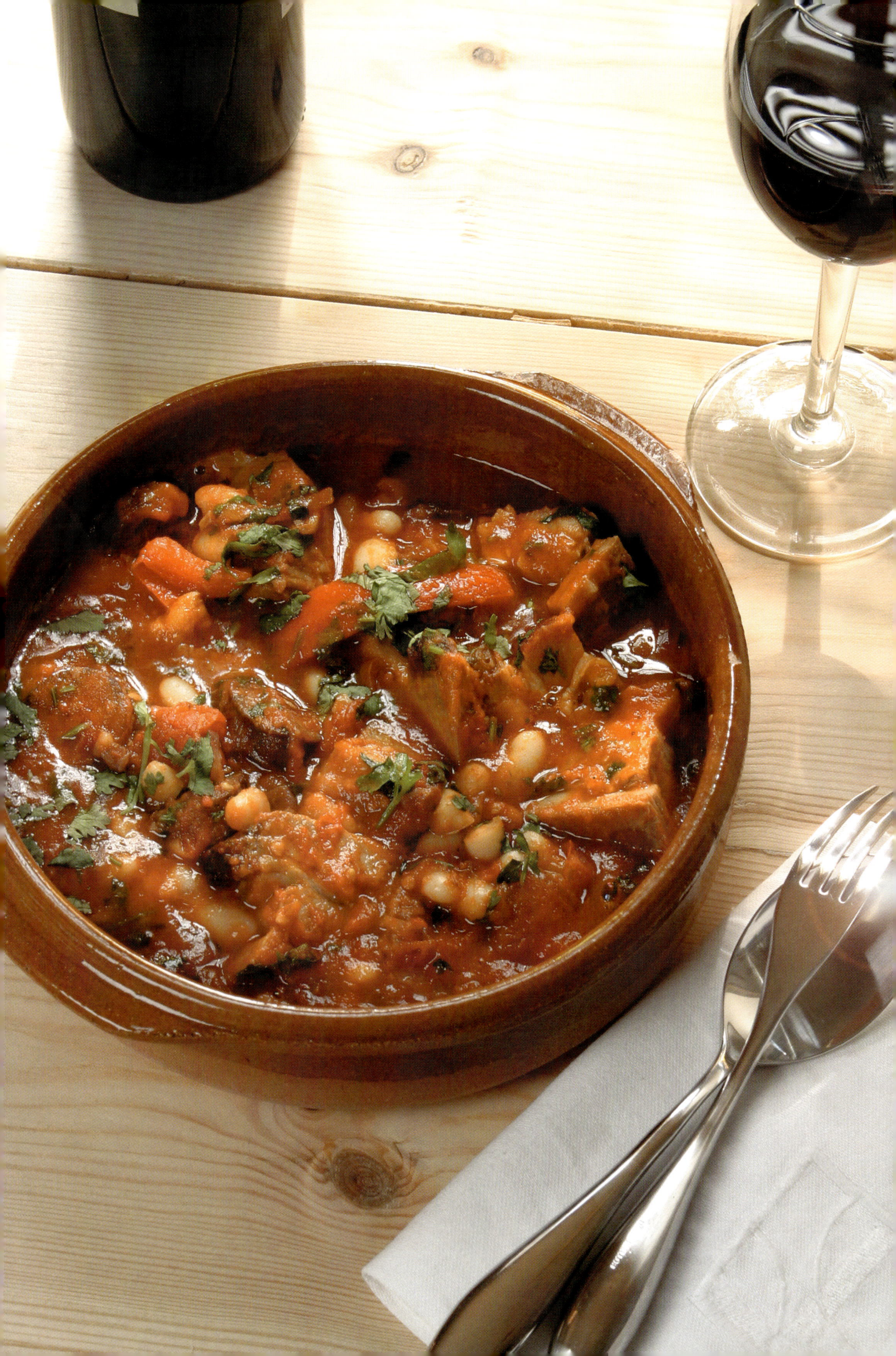

CAFÉ CULTURE

WHOLE ROAST SEA BASS
with Lyonnaise potatoes and salsa verde

Sea bass is an absolutely wonderful fish. While it's true that in recent times it's lost some of its previous exclusivity – you'll often see people buying these to cook at home now – this shouldn't detract from the fact that the flavour you can get from sea bass is something to be treasured. Though it has a lovely shiny, silver appearance when fresh, the flesh inside is a beautiful, stark pristine white. At least, it has when it's fresh. You really need to be a little wary when out shopping for sea bass. Take a look at the fish's eyes; if they shine, the fish is fresh, but if they're dull it's less likely to be so. And freshness is directly related to the quality of flavour you're likely to get. Find a catch of good ones though, and you have yourself the ideal (and relatively stress-free) dinner party dish. You can fit six on an oven tray and prepare them beforehand, ready for putting in the oven. Sea bass works especially well when combined with salsa verde. **AC**

INGREDIENTS

4 whole sea bass (350g each), gutted and scaled
4 large garlic cloves, sliced
32 sprigs thyme
Salt and pepper
Olive oil

METHOD

1. Pre-heat oven to 200°c.
2. Place the sea bass on a chopping board. Insert a sharp knife into the fillets, four times on each fish, cutting through to the bone.
3. Insert two sprigs of thyme and one slice of garlic into each cut.
4. Season with salt and pepper.
5. Place on a flat tray, and pour the olive oil over the fish.
6. Place into the oven, bake for about 12 minutes, and serve.

TO SERVE

Serve with a wedge of lemon, salsa verde (see Extra Thyme), Lyonnaise potatoes (see Extra Thyme)

CHEF'S TIPS

Quite often, you'll get whole fish home only to find that there are a few troublesome scales remaining on the fish. Like wood, fish have a grain running down them, and it's this that you need to bear in mind while preparing to de-scale. Always go from the fish's tail up towards the head, against the grain, and use the back of a chef's knife to de-scale. It's easier to do it the fresher the fish is, so don't just leave it for later as that will only cause problems. The whole trick with the dish is again down to good preparation, and in not over-complicating good, simple, effective flavours. **RS**

RECOMMENDED WINE

4

Meursault

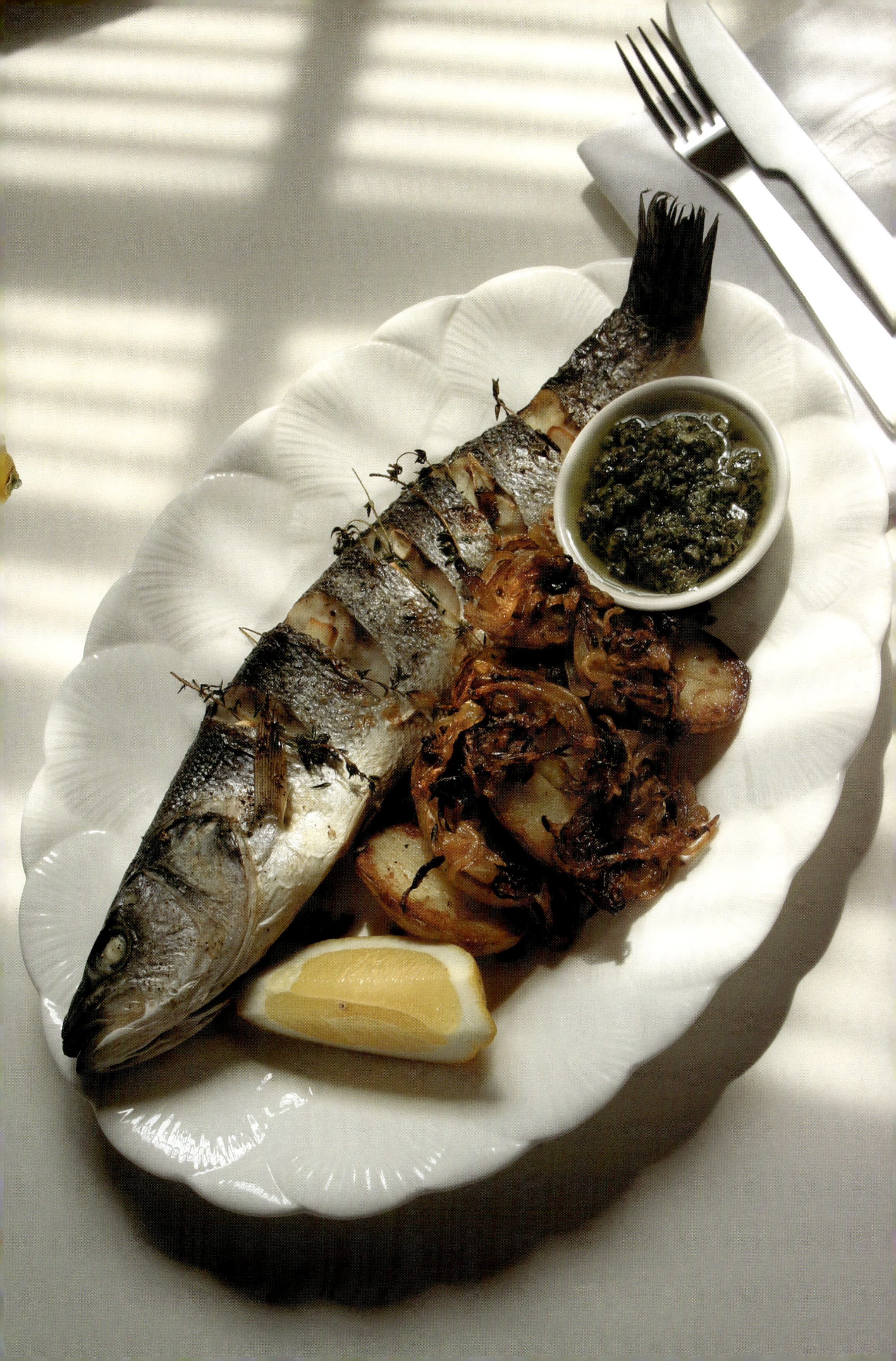

CAFÉ CULTURE

LINGUINE
with garlic, lemon, chilli and rocket

Ah Bellessima! A glass of Chianti Classico in hand, you relax on the terrace to watch the sun go down over the Tuscan landscape. The smell of cooking is carried over on the perfumed air. In the evening haze you can just make out, in the middle distance, the towers and spires of Siena, while closer to you, the rows of vineyards dominate the landscape… then you wake up and you're still in Sheffield. Never mind. This dish may not be quite the equivalent of a trip to Italy, but it certainly evokes the taste of the real thing. **RS**

INGREDIENTS
100-120ml extra virgin olive oil
2 red chillis, diced
3 large garlic cloves, chopped
Grated zest of ½ lemon
1 lemon, juice only
1 packet dried linguine

METHOD
1 Cook the linguine in plenty of salted boiling water until tender.
2 Meanwhile, heat the olive oil in a saucepan, add garlic, lemon and chilli, and gently fry, releasing all the flavours without colouring.
3 Toss the linguine in with the chilli mix.
4 Add the dressed rocket, and serve immediately with plenty of grated parmesan.

TO SERVE
dressed wild rocket (approx. 20g each)
freshly grated parmesan

CHEF'S TIPS
I've said it before and I'll say it again. Don't worry if your pasta dishes are fairly sparse on the sauce. That's the way it should be. The important thing is that they don't lack anything in flavour.

We serve this at the café regularly, in the authentic Italian style. As long as you follow the basic principles of a pasta dish, don't be afraid to experiment a little with the ingredients. This is great on its own but also lends itself well to many variations. Sometimes we add chargrilled courgettes. Go with whatever takes your fancy or whatever needs using up in the fridge. But go easy on the quantities. **AC**

RECOMMENDED WINE

Pinot Grigio Alpha zeta

THYME AFTER THYME

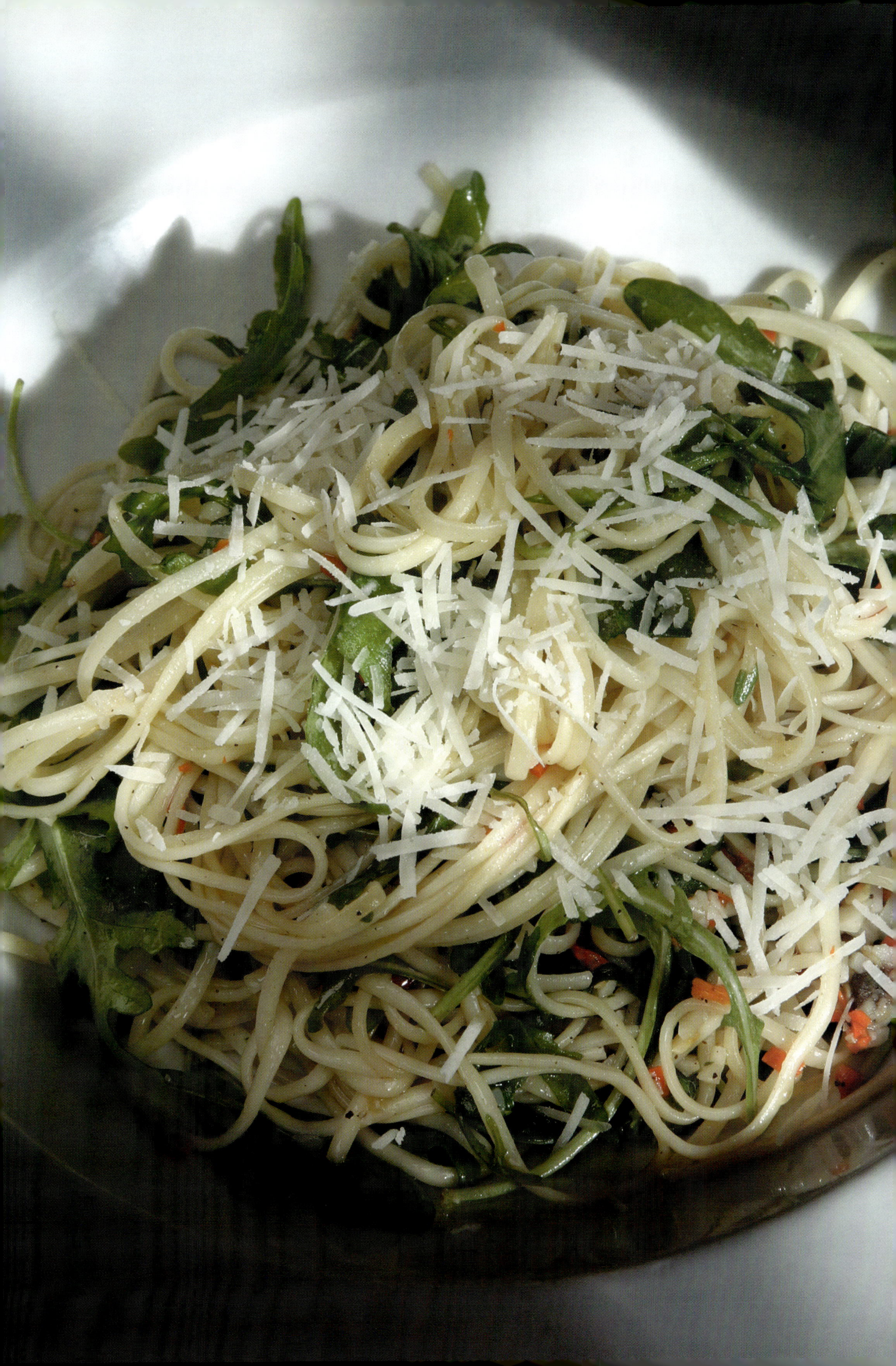

CHAPTER 2
CLASSICS

CLASSICS

SCALLOPS
with fennel remoulade and watercress

There is little to compare with good quality scallops properly cooked. The pity is, I can't think of a food that is more abused. At Thyme, we insist on using only hand-dived scallops. The alternative is the dredged variety, which in my book come a very poor second. The problem is that the dredging process brings up everything else with it, so your shellfish end up full of whatever was on the seabed. Just as bad, scallops sold by weight are sometimes soaked in water. They soak it up like a sponge, and end up tasting more like a squash ball after cooking. The moral is, unless you're splashing out on the very best quality scallops available, don't bother. That said, this dish has to be one of my all-time favourites. The aniseed sharpness of the fennel is the perfect partner to the delicate flavour of the scallops. **RS**

INGREDIENTS
500g fresh scallops
4 rashers of streaky bacon (optional)
100g mayonnaise
Juice of 1 lemon
250g finely shaved fennel
Small bunch chopped flat parsley
Salt
Pepper
Dressed watercress

METHOD
1. Finely slice the fennel down a mandolin.
2. In a bowl, combine with the mayonnaise, lemon juice, parsley, salt and pepper.
3. Wrap the scallop in the bacon and season. Fry in a little hot oil for no more than 1–1½ minutes each side.
4. The scallops should be nicely browned on the outside yet opaque in the centre.

TO SERVE
1. Spoon out the fennel remoulade into the centre of the plate.
2. Arrange the scallops around it and top the fennel with dressed watercress.
3. Drizzle a little extra virgin olive oil.

CHEF'S TIPS
All right, so you're armed with some good quality scallops. Round one is won. The fennel remoulade is a doddle (yes, it is the same thing as coleslaw, but it always sounds better in French, doesn't it?). However, since we lived in litigious times, just let me warn you to be careful with the mandolin. I have had, and witnessed, some accidents in the kitchen you really do not want to hear about. The health warning over, there is just one more golden rule with scallops. Whatever happens, don't be tempted to overcook them – they are really poor eating if you do. Use a medium heat, not too much oil and employ an iron discipline to take them out of the pan as soon as the stated time has elapsed and they are nicely brown on the outside. You will be richly rewarded with the result. **RS**

RECOMMENDED WINES
3 4
Puligny Montrachet

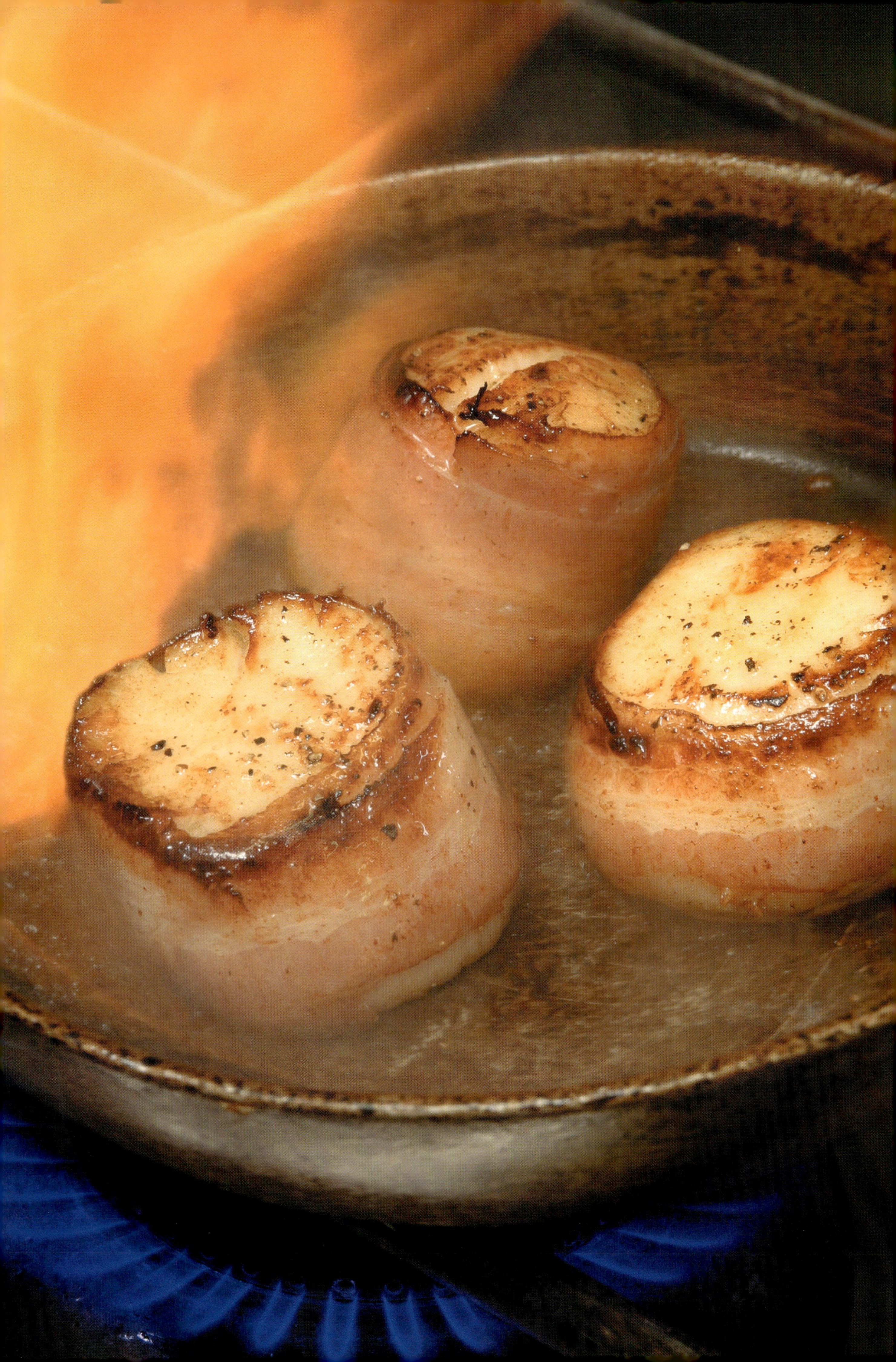

CLASSICS

ROAST BEEF
and Yorkshire pudding

I'm sure that for everyone, certain foods evoke certain special memories. For many people reading this, this dish will take them back to a time when they'd spend Sundays with the family; mother hard at work, hunched over a stove to prepare a big roast dinner, aunts fussing round in the kitchen being generally unhelpful, and everyone else sitting in the living room watching the big match on television. The food was usually a letdown. The vegetables were overcooked, as was the beef. I used to prefer to be off playing football with my mates. Now, I miss the whole family aspect of it. The French love to make a big deal about eating as a family, but it seems to be something that's drifted out of our culture. Hopefully, dishes like this will help steer us back to a more traditional way of doing things. As for the food itself, it's again very much down to getting hold of good ingredients. Always opt for meat that is extra mature and has been hung longer, as this brings out the best in the beef. For full benefit in terms of flavour it should be rare roasted. **AC**

INGREDIENTS
1 x 2–2.5kg sirloin beef
Vegetable oil
Salt and pepper
1 batch Yorkshire puddings (see Extra Thyme)
1 batch roast potatoes (see Extra Thyme)
1 batch Vichy carrots (see Extra Thyme)
1 batch honey roast parsnips (see Extra Thyme)
1 batch French beans Lyonnaise (see Extra Thyme)
1 carrot
1/2 onion
2 garlic cloves
2 celery sticks
3 sprigs of Thyme
1 litre brown chicken stock

METHOD
1. Pre heat oven to 190°C
2. Score the fat on top of the beef and season with salt and pepper.
3. Heat a large roasting tray on the cooker top and seal the beef on all sides.
4. Place in the oven, turning regularly so it is eventually cooked. A 2kg sirloin should take 1¼ – 1½ hours.
5. Roughly chop the onion, carrot and celery, garlic and thyme and add to the roasting tray halfway through cooking and stir from time to time to prevent burning.
6. To check the meat is ready, insert a sharp knife into the centre of the joint and leave for 30 seconds. Remove and the knife should be warm, the more you like the meat cooking the hotter the knife should be.
7. When you have cooked the beef to your liking, remove from the roasting tray, wrap in foil and leave to rest for 30 minutes.
8. Pour out any excess fat from the roasting tray and add the brown chicken stock. Bring to boil and pour into a saucepan and gently simmer for 20 minutes. Pass through a sieve and serve.

CHEF'S TIPS
Make sure to give yourself plenty of time over this one, as you'll reap the rewards of a relaxed, leisurely approach. Rest the meat after cooking for 30 minutes, take it out of the oven and cover it with foil. For some reason it relaxes the meat, and it becomes ever so tender. If it's straight from the oven it can end up being a little chewy and unpleasant. Make sure not to overcook the vegetables, but don't be tempted to do the opposite and go the other way either. Vegetables should have some bite, but undercooked they are just as unpalatable as when overcooked, which is something modern restaurants often ignore. If you want to deviate a little from tradition, try making up some horseradish mash – it's a superb accompaniment. **RS**

RECOMMENDED WINE

Journeys End Ascent Shiraz/ Barossa Shiraz

THYME AFTER THYME

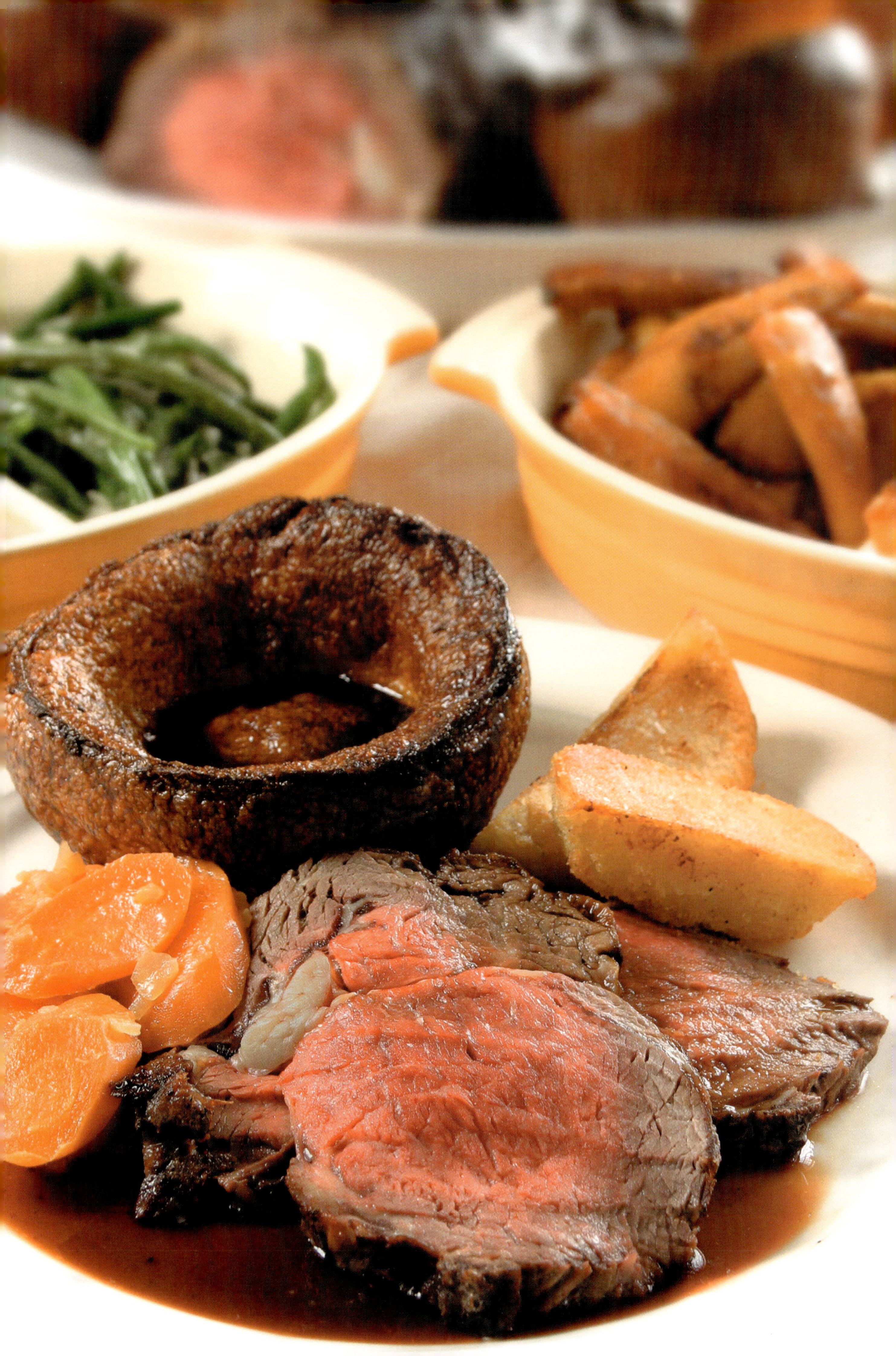

CLASSICS

ONION TART
with manchego cheese

Ah, Manchego! Could only be Spanish, couldn't it? Even if you fluffed a multiple-choice question asking whether Manchego was (a) A traditional dance, (b) A well-known flamenco guitarist or (c) A leading exponent of modern art, bet you'd pick the right country on the map when asked to pinpoint its origin. The answer is in fact (d) A Spanish ewe's milk cheese, pale, with a fairly hard texture and a black rind. We use it in a variety of dishes at Thyme, few of them to greater effect that in this simple-to-prepare, but quite delicious tart. **AC**

INGREDIENTS
120g grated manchego cheese
1 blind baked tartlet case
   (see extra thyme)

Onion mix
 3 large thinly-sliced onions
125g butter
25g plain flour
Salt
Pepper
Pinch of sugar

Egg mixture
3 eggs
150 ml cream
150 ml milk
Salt
Pepper

METHOD
1 Heat a large saucepan and melt the butter.
2 Add the sliced onions, salt, pepper and pinch of sugar.
3 Cook the onions down over low to medium heat for 20–25 minutes, stirring from time to time to prevent burning.
4 When they are lightly browned, stir in the flour and cook for a couple of minutes.
5 Reserve mixture.
6 Whisk the eggs and milk together with a little salt and pepper.
7 Fill the blind-baked pastry shell with the onion mixture.
8 Top with the grated manchego cheese.
9 Put the egg mixture into a jug and pour onto the tart.
10 Bake in a preheated oven (180°c) for 25–30 minutes.
11 Leave to cool for 30 minutes to1 hour before serving.

TO SERVE
1 Cut the tart into 4–6 good sized wedges.
2 Serve with hot buttered new potatoes and a crisp green salad.

CHEF'S TIPS
When you roll out the pastry, let it rest in the tin. Pop it in the fridge for an hour or so, then add the baking beans or rice prior to it going in the oven. I'm man enough to admit I'm not the greatest pastry chef in the world. The craft of the skilled pastry chef is an art in itself. But this is a tart anyone can make. That's because there's a little insurance policy built into the dish in case of mishap. The chief danger is that your pastry case might end up with a hole in it somewhere. If so, don't worry (unless the breach is reminiscent of a good night's work by the Dambusters). The egg mixture will cook quickly, setting and sealing any leaks in the tart – unlike mixtures such as lemon tart filling, for example, which will end up on the floor, on the base of the oven and over your shoes too. One more tip; save any unused pastry. Use it to line moulds, freeze them, and they're ready for use next time. **AC**

RECOMMENDED WINES

3

Eden Valley Viognier

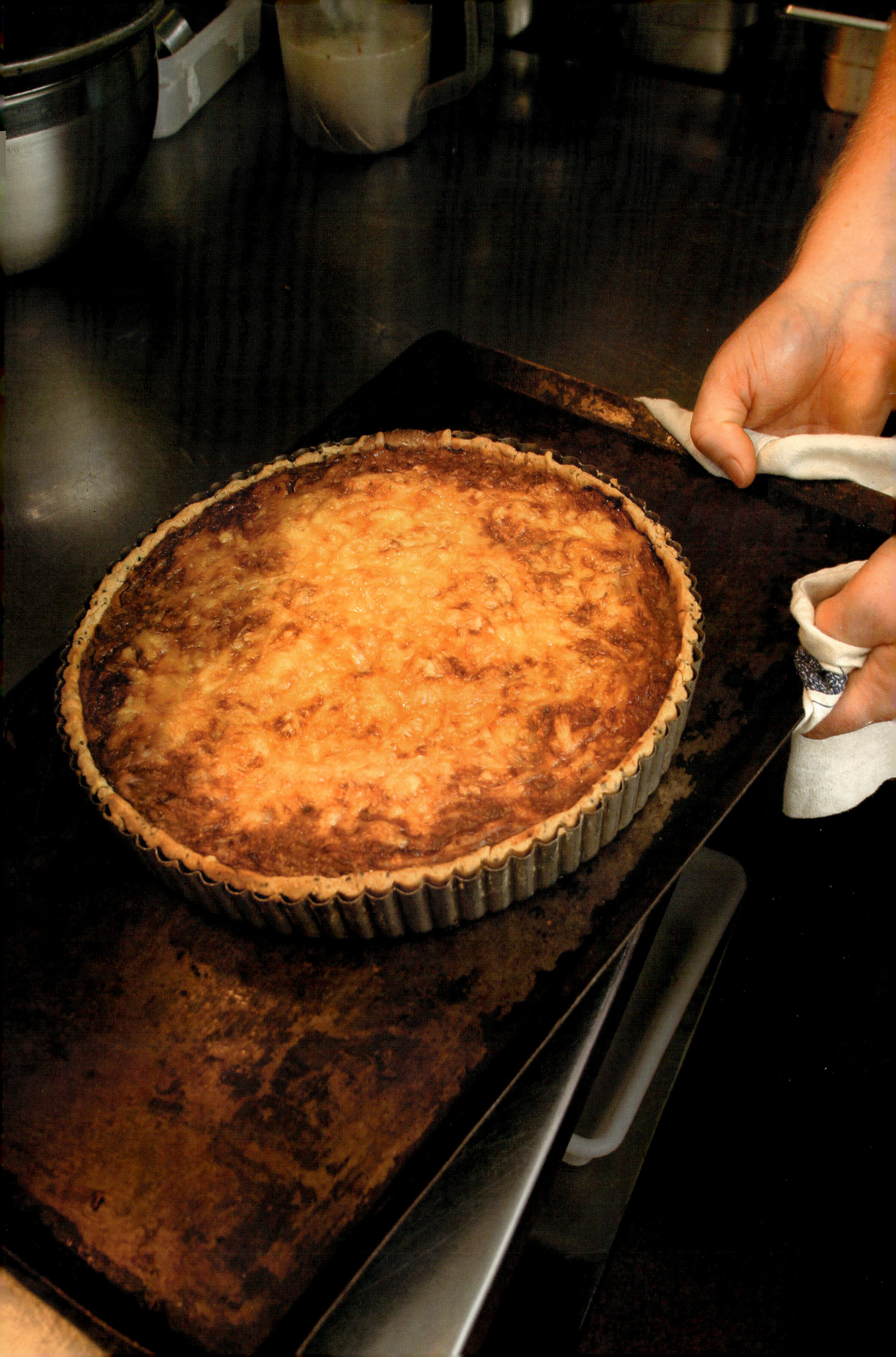

CLASSICS

FISH AND CHIPS

I prefer not to get worked up into too much of a frenzy about this whole concept of 'New English Cooking'. There are always those sorts of people who are obsessed with labels like this, but they generally tend not to be the ones who are actually out there coming up with exciting, worthwhile new innovations. More often than not, they are dragging themselves up on the coat-tails of this week's particular trend. Fashion has its place in the industry, but good food is about what you like eating. And this, I have to say, has always been one of my favourite meals. Like everyone, I've done my fair share of visits to the chip shop, and what you end up with isn't always that cracking – all too often it was a tale of soggy batter, rock-hard fish and last week's heated-up mushy peas. Luckily, my dad used to cook up a mean fish and chips at home, and that's the sort of thing I'm trying to emulate here. This is a dish that's part of our national identity, so I think it's important to see it done well. Even as recently as 10 years ago, food critics would have been amazed had they come across this on a menu, but now it's more accepted. Some may place it in a particular category, but I prefer to enjoy it for what it is. **AC**

INGREDIENTS

1kg skinless boneless cod or haddock fillet
Plain flour (for coating)
Salt and pepper

Batter
180g plain flour
90g self raising flour
220ml beer (chilled)
1 egg yolk
200ml semi skimmed milk
25ml vegetable oil
Salt and pepper

METHOD

1 Pre-heat the deep fryer to 170°c.
2 Mix the batter ingredients together until it forms a smooth paste.
3 Portion the fish, making sure it has no bones.
4 Flour the fish, and season with salt and pepper.
5 Dip the fish into the batter mix, making sure it is completely covered. Let any excess batter drip off.
6 Place the fish into the fryer, making sure that they don't stick together or to the bottom of the fryer.
7 Cook the fish until the batter is crispy (this should take around 5 minutes).
8 When the fish is ready, remove from the fryer and place on kitchen towels to get rid of any excess fat.
9 Serve with chips, tartare sauce, mushy peas, lemon wedges, and, if you can manage it, bread and butter.

TO SERVE

Chips (see Extra Thyme)
Lemon wedges
Tartare sauce (see Extra Thyme)
Mushy peas (see Extra Thyme)
Bread and butter

CHEF'S TIPS

Just about everyone has their own personal recipe for batter, but I find that this one works best because it gives you that oh-so-desirable crispness. It's important to ensure the batter isn't too thick, otherwise it will go soft and gooey on the inside – ideally, your batter should be light-crisp and golden brown. Believe it or not, I've seen people actually stripping off the batter, leaving themselves with the fish only. It makes good sense really, as the fish is actually perfectly steamed – but really, biting into the batter forms a large part of the dish's charm. As for the choice of fish, it's really down to personal choice. For me, you can't really top using the tail ends of cod. There's one major danger to look out for. During cooking, keep the fish moving to avoid it sticking. If it sticks, the batter breaks, oil gets in the fish, you have an awful, soggy result and someone has to be sent out to the local chippie. **RS**

RECOMMENDED WINES

1

Champagne

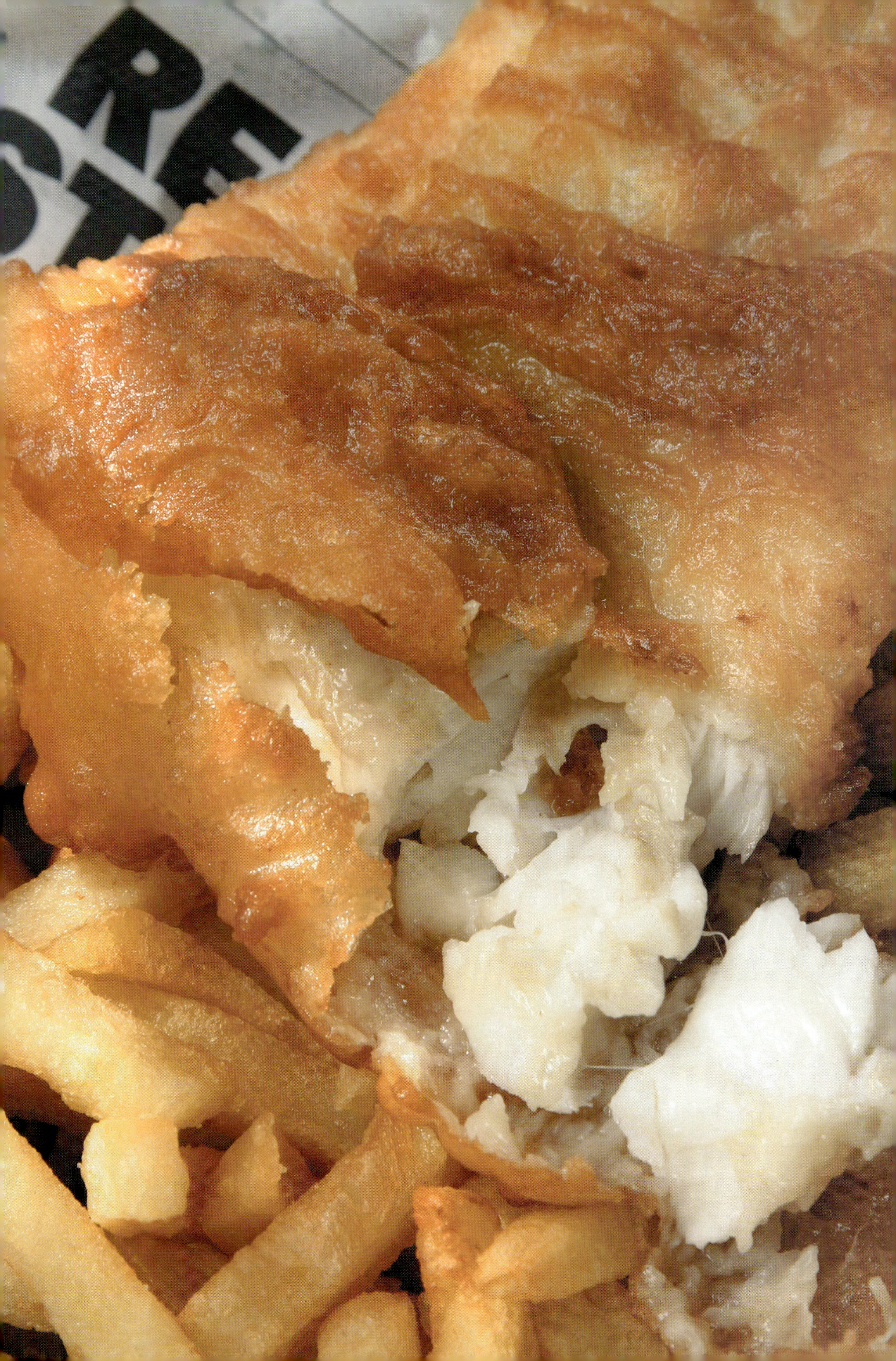

CLASSICS

FIG & MOZZARELLA BRUSCHETTA

Let's hear it for the Italians! They may not be the supreme power in football any longer, but when it comes to a bit of inspired basic thinking in the kitchen, they win hands down. Bruschetta, like many of the most inspired dishes ever created, was the answer to a simple problem – what to do with all that stale bread? We Brits, by contrast, decided to put it in bread and butter pudding, but then the other lot did start with a decided advantage… endless supplies of full-flavoured olive oil, the best-tasting tomatoes in the world, pungent fresh basil… the list goes on. All in all, it's a cook's dream team. **AC**

INGREDIENTS

1 ready to bake ciabatta loaf
4 ripe fresh figs
2 buffalo mozzarella
1 peeled clove garlic
50ml olive oil
Dressed rocket
Parmesan shavings

METHOD

1. Cut the ciabatta into 8 thick slices, rub with olive oil and chargrill or fry in a pan if you don't have a chargrill pan.
2. Quarter the figs.
3. Slice the mozzarella.
4. Dress the rocket and shave the parmesan.

TO SERVE

1. Place 2 pieces of chargrilled bread in the centre of the plate.
2. Top with the figs and mozzarella slices.
3. Pile the dressed rocket on top and shave the parmesan with a vegetable peeler.

CHEF'S TIPS

Here's a dish that exemplifies what the Italians do best – simple cooking and forget the frills. Don't worry if you haven't any Ciabatta. Indeed, one of the best Italian cooks I know uses French bread. I often eat her bruschetta and marvel that nothing more than a combination of bread, tomatoes and oil can taste so good. The great thing about bruschetta is that you can enjoy it with endless different toppings. Try our version with sliced parma ham for a change. Figs are really at their best in the autumn. They should be a dark almost purpley colour, soft to touch and a vibrant red colour inside. **RS**

RECOMMENDED WINES

Sancerre 2/3

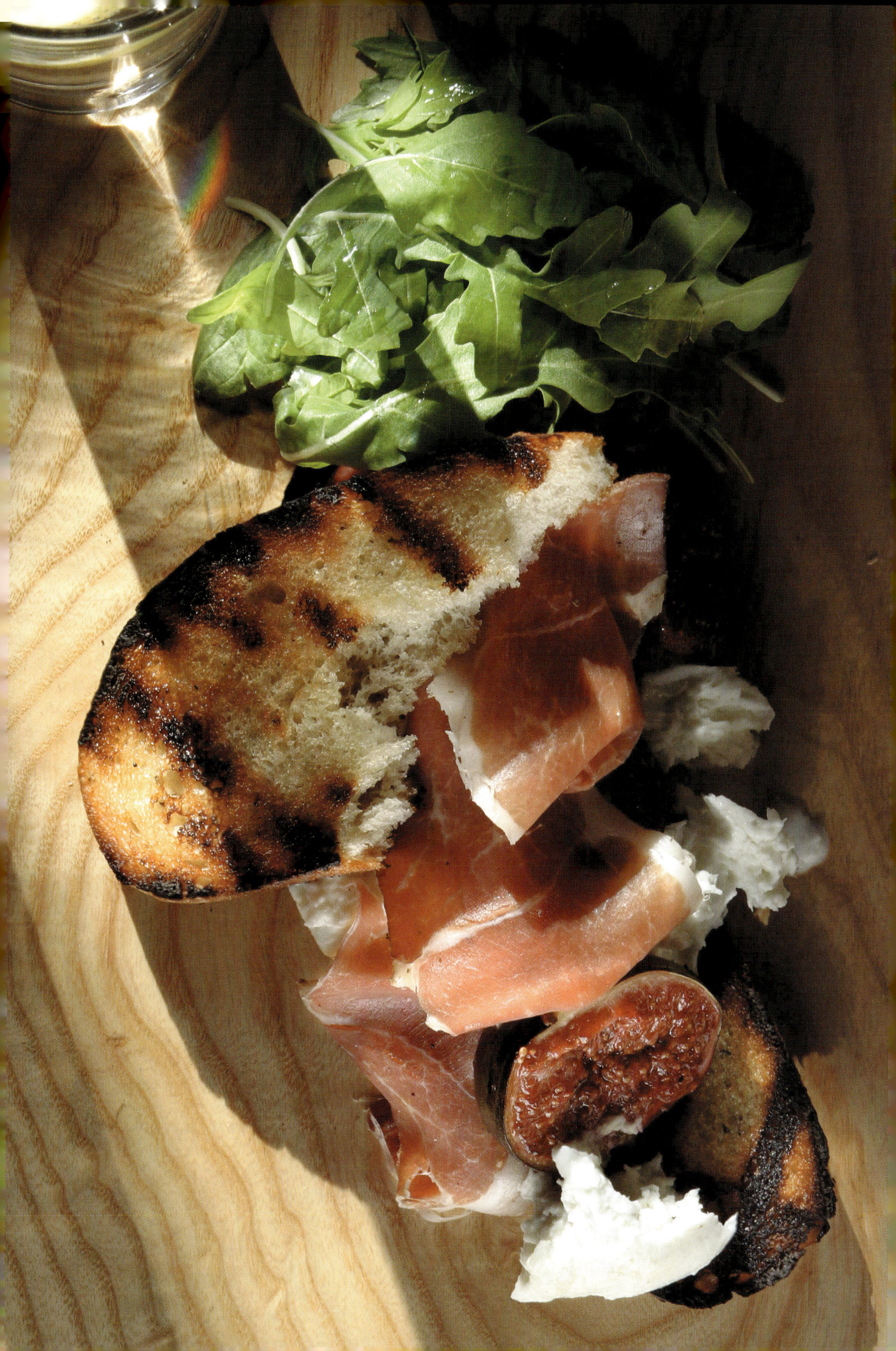

CLASSICS

MUSSELS
with garlic cream sauce

Mussels are much more than just a national dish in Belgium. They are virtually a national symbol, and their seasonal arrival always seems to cause great excitement when I'm over there. A lot of it could be down to the world-famous beers that Belgium also produces; after all, mussels and beer are a marriage made in heaven. We've called it 'mussels in garlic cream sauce' but its essentially a mariniere, of which there are many different versions. For example, Richard thinks there shouldn't be cream in the dish, whereas I personally like it. It really doesn't matter, as this is a dish that's very adaptable. You can do a Thai version with garlic, chilli and coriander, a curried Indian effort, or you could even try one with a beer and bacon sauce. **AC**

INGREDIENTS
1 large onion, chopped
1 large carrot, finely diced
1 large celery stick, finely diced
4 large garlic cloves, crushed
2 bay leaves
Bunch fresh thyme
300ml white wine
2kg fresh mussels, de-bearded and washed
Small bunch flat leaf parsley, chopped
200ml double cream

METHOD
1. De-beard, trim and wash the mussels, discarding any that are open or cracked.
2. In a large hot saucepan add the wine, chopped vegetables, bay leaf and thyme.
3. Bring to the boil and add the mussels.
4. Place a lid on top of the pan and keep shaking the pan around.
5. Cook for about 5 minutes, until all the shells are open.
6. Add the double cream, return to the boil, sprinkle with chopped parsley and serve immediately in a large moules pot or deep-sided serving dish.

ASSEMBLY
Serve with a bucket of fries, a basket of crusty bread, a pot of garlic mayonnaise, and a glass of De Koninck. This is a great dish to serve and eat communally with family and friends.

TO SERVE
Bucket of fries
Crusty bread
Garlic mayo
Finger bowl

CHEF'S TIPS
There's a very simple rule to follow when buying mussels: only purchase them when there's an 'R' in the month. In other words, leave well alone during the summer. Only ever use fresh mussels, and avoid the New Zealand green lip variety. Unfortunately, they have a poor appearance and are chewy and over-large. Make sure you wash the mussels well, and don't, whatever else you do, overcook them. There's nothing worse than tough, shrunken mussels that have lost the plumpness that makes them so appetising in the first place. Discard any mussels that are open after the initial washing process, or that don't open after cooking – they could be toxic – and make sure to serve them the day you buy them to take maximum advantage of their sweet, salty taste. **RS**

RECOMMENDED WINES

1 2

Muscadet

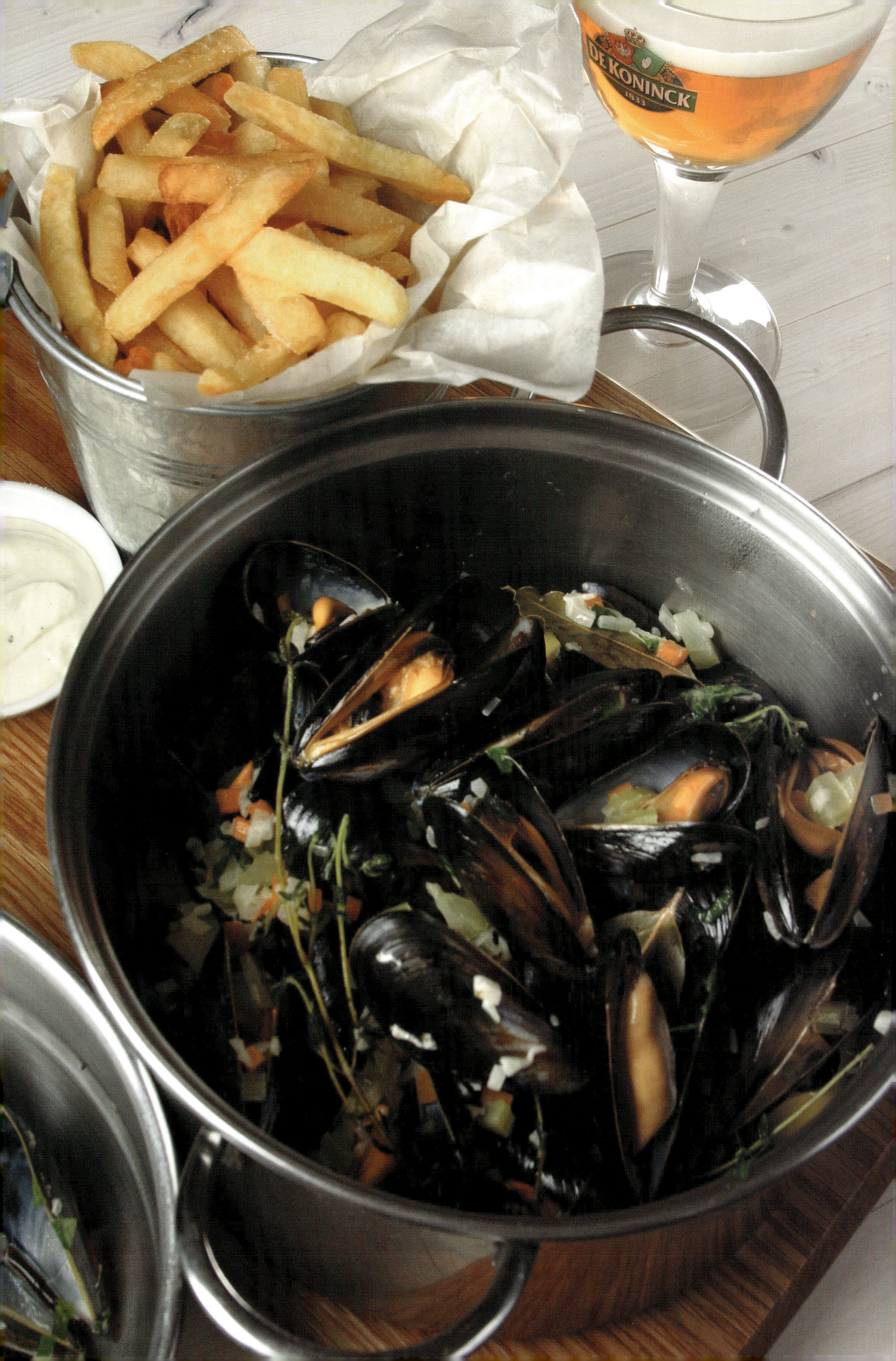
DE KONINCK
1833

CLASSICS

BRAISED LAMB SHANKS
with root vegetable mash

Here's a dish that's as traditionally English as the village cricket match and morris dancing. Or, quite possibly, even more so. This really has proved to be an enduring favourite at Thyme Café, where it's been an ever-present on the menu. There aren't any hidden surprises, so customers know exactly what they're getting: ever-so tender meat that gently falls off the bone, and wonderful, complementary vegetables. The essence of the dish is in the way the lamb is cooked. Good things tend to come to those who wait, and the slow-braising process really entices the maximum flavour out of the lamb. **AC**

INGREDIENTS
- 4 lamb shanks
- 1 large onion
- 2 large carrots
- 3 celery sticks
- 1 garlic bulb
- 1 bunch thyme
- 1 bunch rosemary
- Salt and pepper
- 2 litres brown chicken stock (or gravy)
- 500ml water
- 60g tomato puree
- 2 bay leaves
- 1 batch root vegetable mash (see Extra Thyme)
- 1 batch French beans Lyonnaise (optional, see Extra Thyme)

METHOD
1. Pre-heat oven to 180°c.
2. Peel and roughly chop the onions, carrots, celery and garlic.
3. In a large saucepan, heat a little vegetable oil and sweat down the vegetables for 10 minutes.
4. Add the tomato puree, cook out, then add the thyme, rosemary, chicken stock and water. Bring to the boil, and reduce to a simmer.
5. Season the lamb shanks with salt and pepper, and seal in a frying pan, ensuring they are nicely browned on each side.
6. Place the lamb shanks into the stock, ensuring they are totally immersed in the liquid.
7. Place a tight-fitting lid (or tin foil) over the top, and place in the oven for around 3 hours.
8. When the lamb is ready, separate the meat from the sauce.
9. Pass the sauce through a sieve, squeezing all the juices from the vegetables. You should be left with what is a luscious piece of lamb-tasting gravy, flavoured with garlic, thyme and rosemary.

TO SERVE
Place the pieces of lamb in the oven with a knob of butter on each, and heat through for around 15 minutes. Place the hot root vegetable mash in the centre of the plate, put a lamb shank on top and pour the lamb gravy over it. This dish eats really well with French beans Lyonnaise.

CHEF'S TIPS
While the lamb by itself is chock-full of flavour, it never hurts to give it an added kick through the judicious addition of rosemary and garlic. How to go about it: before the meat is sealed, which naturally takes place during the cooking process, place a knife down the side of the bone and carefully dot a few incisions. Stuff in as much rosemary and garlic as you and your dining companions can take, sit back and relax with a newspaper, and prepare to look smug when it's time to serve it up. **RS**

RECOMMENDED WINES

5

Bourgogne Pinot Noir

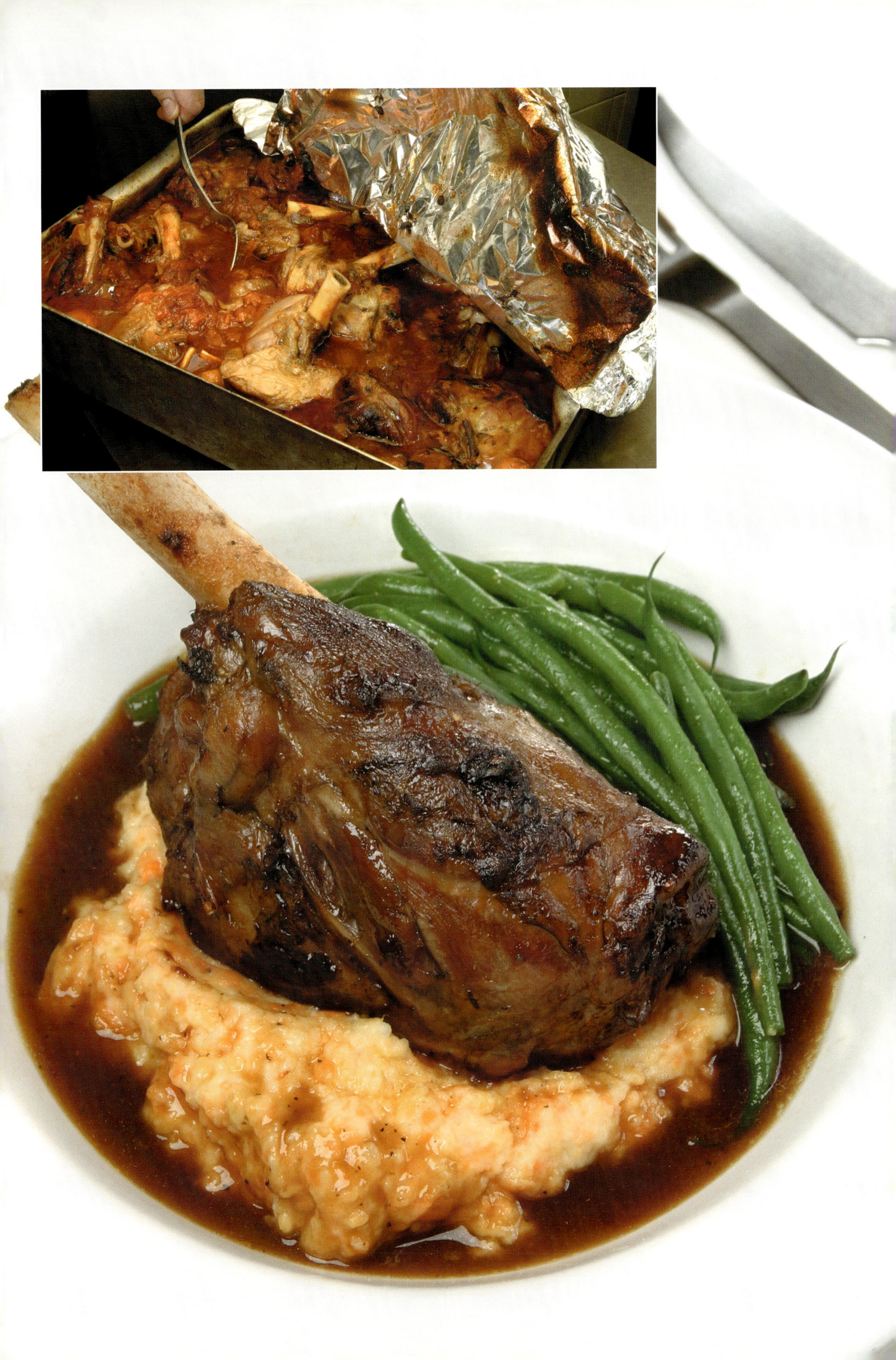

CLASSICS

MEAT AND POTATO PIE

As two Sheffield-based restaurants, it's important to reflect the locality we operate in, and this is a classic dish using two ingredients that are synonymous with the city: Henderson's Relish and Stones Bitter. It's the perfect dish to serve up on a cold evening. On a winter's day, with the long, frost-bitten walks home from school, I remember often getting back so cold I couldn't move a muscle. But the warming prospect of the meat and potato pie that awaited never failed to work wonders. Unfortunately, it's the sort of thing we don't tend to make any more; people seem to prefer to buy the microwaveable version. I saw a statistic recently that stated we spend an average of 15 minutes a day cooking, and that really is a shame. Dishes like this one are much simpler and quicker to make than you'd first think, and invariably prove to be a hit with the lucky recipient. Meat and potato pie is what home-style cooked food is all about, and it has proved to be one of the most popular dishes at the Café. **AC**

INGREDIENTS

Meat mix
2kg lean braising steak, diced
2 x 440 ml cans of Stones bitter
2 bay leaves
bunch thyme (tied with string)
3 litres beef stock (or stock cubes & water)
80g brown sauce
100ml Henderson's Relish
50g butter
60g plain flour
1.3kg potatoes, peeled and diced

Pastry
200g self raising flour
200g plain flour
100g Atora suet
85g butter
Pinch salt
60ml water

METHOD

1. Place the braising steak in a large saucepan.
2. Cover in beer and stock, and add the salt and pepper.
3. Bring to boil and reduce to a simmer.
4. Add the bay leaf and thyme, and cook for about 2 hours until the meat is tender.
5. Add the peeled, diced potatoes and cook gently until the potatoes are soft and about to fall.
6. Stir in the Henderson's Relish and brown sauce.
7. Melt the butter in the microwave and stir in the flour until a smooth paste is formed.
8. Stir this into the pie mix until the gravy is nicely coating the back of a spoon.

Pastry
1. Mix the flours, suet, butter and salt together until a breadcrumb texture is achieved.
2. Add water until mixture comes together and forms a dough. Wrap it in cling film and place in fridge for 30 minutes to rest.
3. Pre-heat the oven to 180°c.
4. When you're ready to use it, bring the pastry out of fridge and soften a little.
5. Roll out (not too thinly) and cut into rounds.
6. Top the pie and bake for about 20 minutes, until the pastry is well browned.

CHEF'S TIPS

The perfect meat and potato pie should literally melt in the mouth. To help create this effect, make sure to roll out the pastry quite thickly. This will help create a soft underside that soaks up the juices from the filling. Try and use just as many potatoes as you do pieces of braising steak, as this will create the right texture and give the correct combination of flavours – but also bear in mind that the addition of Henderson's Relish is also important, giving an extra zip to the filling. Finally, take your time over this one, and give it plenty of chance to cook through so that the flavours can develop fully. **RS**

RECOMMENDED WINES

7

Ch. Glana/Claret

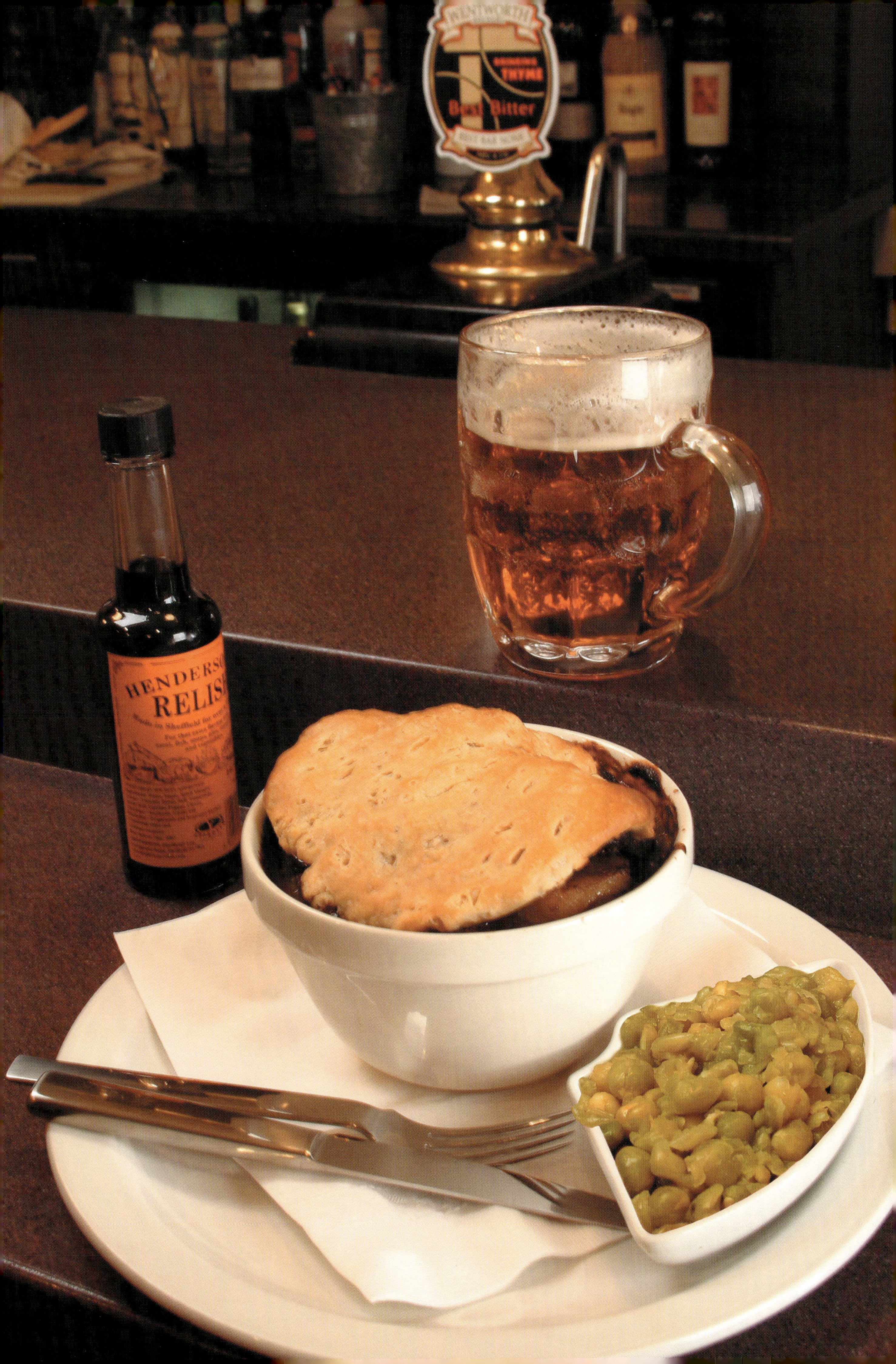
WENTWORTH
THYME
Best Bitter

CLASSICS

FISHCAKES
with Green vegetables & Butter sauce

Let us praise the holy trinity. The humble fishcake is one of the three dishes I revere most, for the simple reason I owe my living to them over the years. This trio – completed by lamb shank and crème brulee – have been my biggest sellers in my time as a restaurant owner. They are popular for the simple reason that people love them. Credit must go to chefs like Phil Vickery, Gary Rhodes and Simon Hopkinson for rediscovering a classic dish and helping it find a place on British menus again. So successful have they been that I now couldn't consider putting on a menu that didn't feature them. Sure, we vary the theme and ingredients, but for me the basic pleasure of eating them remains the same – bite through the crispy coating and savour the fluffy potato and flaked fish within. Perfect. *RS*

INGREDIENTS

Fishcake Mix
600g skinless boneless cod fillet
550g salmon fillet
100ml white wine
Salt and pepper
1kilo potatoes
8–10 finely chopped spring onion
Grated zest of 2 lemons
Small bunch of chopped dill
Small bunch chopped tarragon
Large bunch chopped flat leaf parsley
100g flour
2 beaten eggs
Breadcrumbs

Vegetable Garnish
16 spears peeled asparagus
100g garden peas
100g shelled broad beans
Buttered spinach (see Extra Thyme)
Pea puree (see Extra Thyme)
Lemon sauce (see Extra Thyme)

METHOD

Fishcake
1. Cook the potatoes. Drain and dry out slightly in the oven. Mash thoroughly ensuring there are no lumps.
2. Place the fish in a small roasting tray and pour over the wine. Season, cover with foil and bake in the oven on 180°c for about 10 minutes.
3. When the fish is just cooked remove from the tray and drain off any excess liquid. Flake the fish into chunky pieces.
4. Combine the flaked fish with the mashed potato, lemon zest, seasoning and chopped herbs.
5. Form into cakes in a pastry cutter. I like to make the cakes quite large but if you prefer you can serve smaller ones by halving the quantity of mixture used for each cake.
6. Place the formed fishcakes on a tray lined with greaseproof paper and refrigerate for 3–4 hours until they become firm.
7. The fishcakes are now ready to coat. Take 3 bowls. Fill the first to about halfway with flour, then, place a beaten egg in the second and finally breadcrumbs in the third. Place the fishcake in the flour. Cover lightly, patting off any excess, then immerse completely in the egg mixture.
8. Next transfer to the breadcrumbs bowl and cover completely, patting off any excess. The fishcake is now ready to cook.
10. Place the fishcakes in a deep fryer on 180°c until nicely browned. This should take around 5 minutes. If you make larger fishcakes you will need to place them in the oven for a further 5 minutes to make sure they are hot all the way through. If you don't have a fryer, shallow fry in a frying pan for 1–2 minutes on each side and place on a tray in the oven for 5–10 minutes. The fishcakes are now ready to serve.

Vegetable garnish
1. Blanch the asparagus for 2–3 minutes in boiling water.
2. Add the peas, cook for a further minute then add the shelled broad beans. Drain into a colander, season and scatter around the outside of the plate.
3. Place the buttered spinach in the centre of the plate and top with fishcake. Shape the hot pea puree between 2 spoons to form a quenelle and place on top of the fishcake. Spoon the lemon sauce around the plate and serve straight away.
4. For a restaurant-style finish you can top the fishcake with a gaufrette potato – a thinly sliced potato cut down a mandolin on the fluted blade giving the potato a quarter turn each slice to create a criss-cross effect. These are then deep fried on 180°c for 5 minutes or until lightly brown and crisp.

CHEF'S TIPS

While I was dictating the contents of this particular recipe, one of our editors looked up from his notes and asked why his fishcakes always fell apart when he cooked them. The answer was two-fold; unless you dry the potatoes, then rest the fishcakes in the fridge after they have been shaped, they will indeed tend to disintegrate when they are in the pan. One other important point is to remember to pick over the fish carefully before you assemble the mixture. Ensure any bone or skin is removed. *RS*

RECOMMENDED WINES

3

Chablis

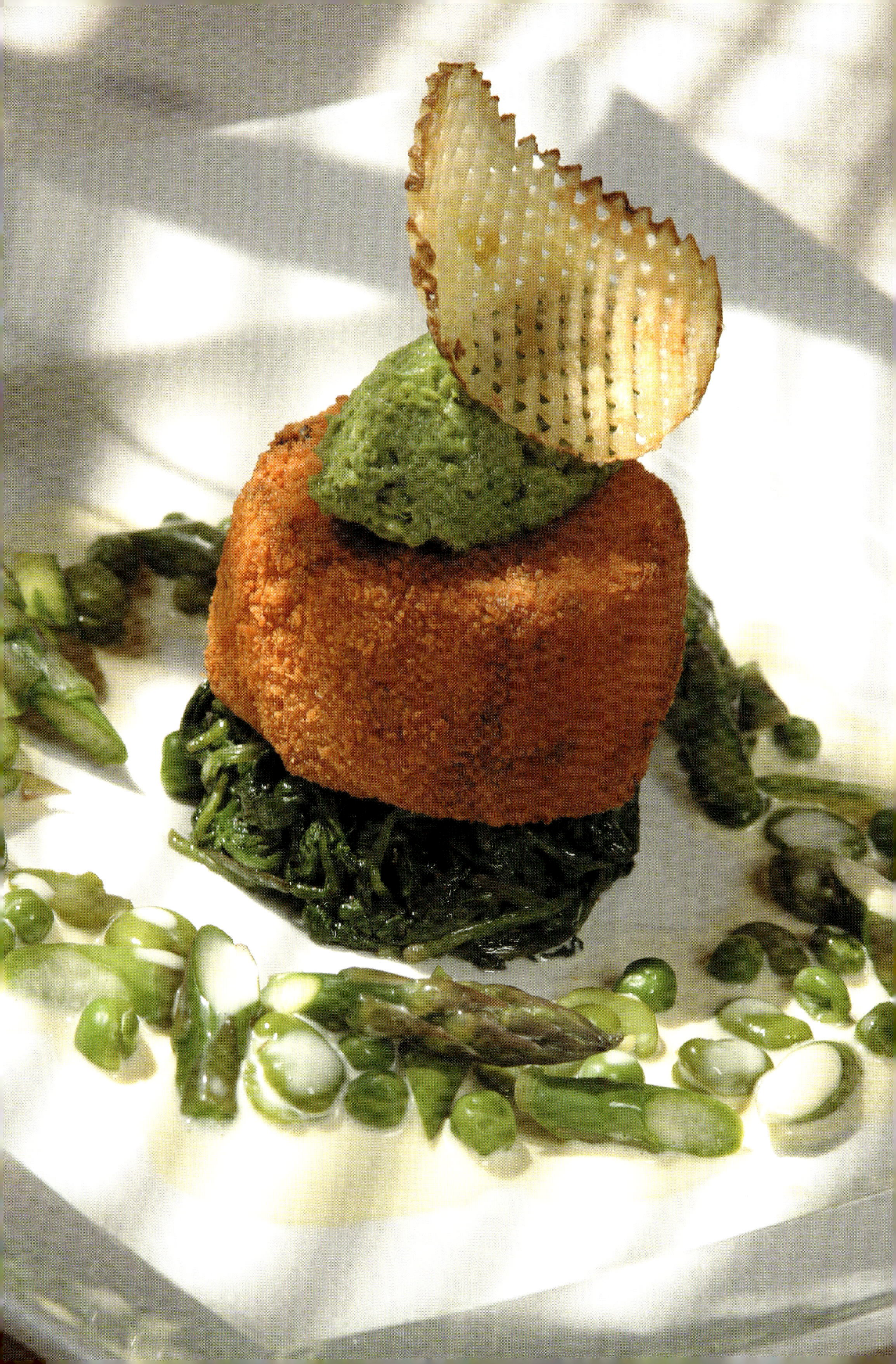

CLASSICS

BOILED HAM HOCK
with grain mustard sauce and spring vegetable mash

If you were to randomly stick a pin in a world atlas, the chances are good that you'd end up selecting a country that possesses its very own version of the ham hock dish. It's such an easy thing to cook that it's hardly surprising the appeal is spread so far and wide. In Germany they dish it up with *sauerkraut*, the Italians incorporate it into a mixed meat plate, while in France you'd find it in *choucroute*. Sadly, here in Britain we're far less imaginative than our cosmopolitan counterparts. We tend to waste our boiled ham by serving it plainly, and it's such a shame. This recipe offers something a little bit more involved, which to my mind does justice to what is undoubtedly a true classic cut of meat. **AC**

INGREDIENTS
4 ham hocks
1 batch spring vegetable mash (see Extra Thyme)

Grain mustard sauce
50g butter
1/2 onion, chopped
125ml white wine
100ml double cream
50g grain mustard

METHOD
1. Place the ham hocks in a large stockpot and cover with water.
2. Bring to the boil, and reduce to a simmer, skimming off any scum that rises to the surface.
3. Make sure that the ham hocks are totally immersed (as the water reduces in volume, keep adding more). The ham should take around 4 hours to cook, and will create a rich stock.
4. When they are ready, serve straight away or leave sitting in the stock until you are ready to eat. It's fine to totally cool down and refrigerate the ham. When you're ready to eat, just bring it slowly back to the boil and serve.

For the sauce
1. Melt the butter in a saucepan.
2. Add the onions and sweat down for 5 minutes, without colouring.
3. Add the white wine, and reduce the liquid by half.
4. Add the ham stock and cook for 5-10 minutes.
5. Add the cream, bring to the boil and stir in the mustard.
6. Check for seasoning, and serve.

TO SERVE
Place the mash in the centre of the plate. Flake the ham hock off the bone and place on top of the mash. Spoon mustard sauce around outside and top with a sprig of parsley

CHEF'S TIPS
It's very much a cliché, but the fact that you've probably heard it a million times before doesn't make it any less true: quality food is only possible with quality ingredients. Sadly, there really is no culinary magic wand that can take a poor cut of meat and transform it into a tender, mouth-watering treat. To make this meal sing, it's vital to buy the ham hock from a good butcher or quality supermarket.

After you've finished boiling the ham, please don't just pour the liquid down the sink. It makes a brilliant stock for that great belly warmer, pea and ham soup. **RS**

RECOMMENDED WINES

6

Luis Canas Reserva Rioja

THYME AFTER THYME

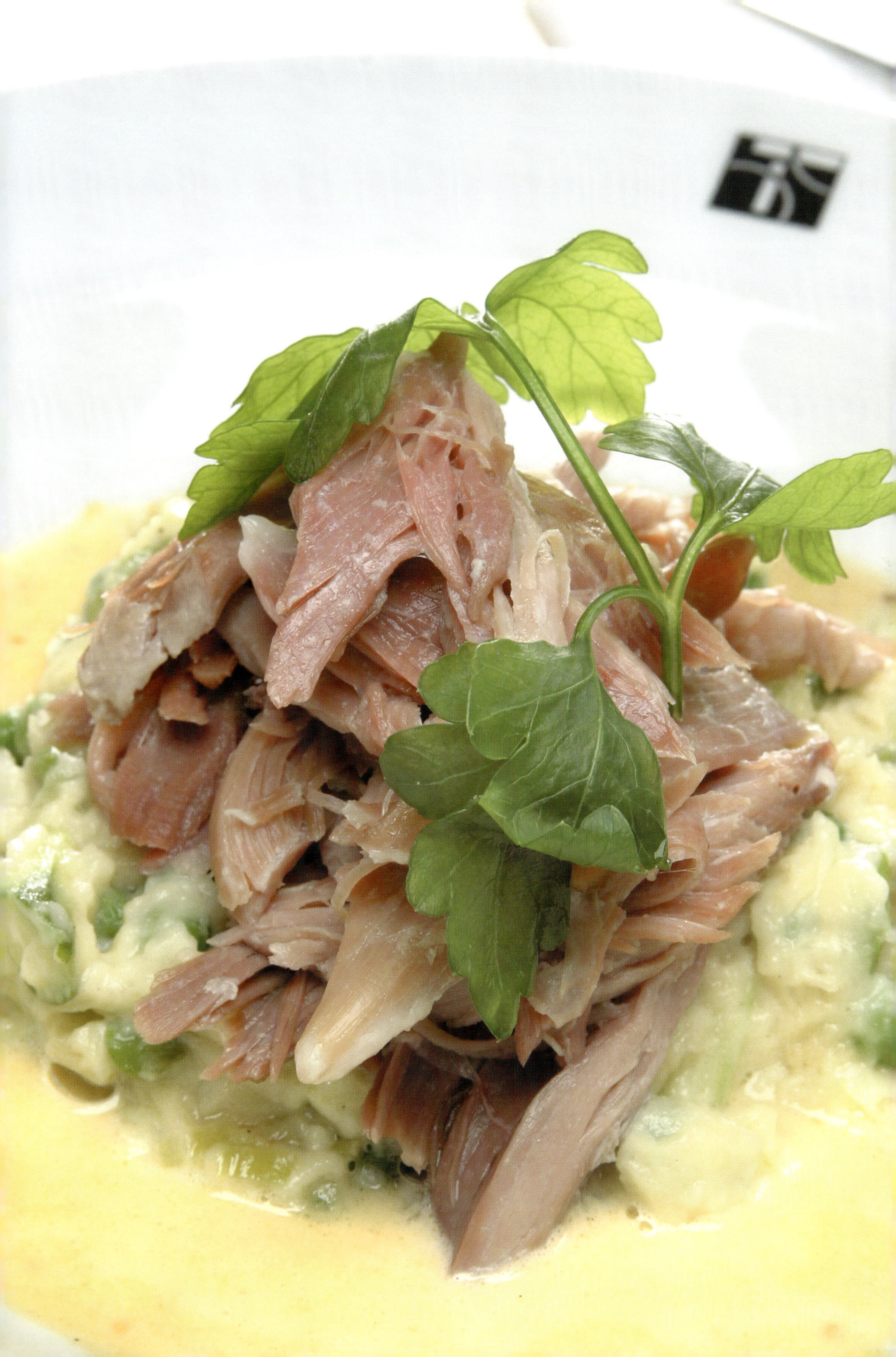

CLASSICS

MARYLAND CRABCAKES
with sweetcorn chowder

There is a story doing the rounds that chowder, that great American eastern shore dish, was actually a British creation imported by the Pilgrim Fathers on the Mayflower. Even if that sounds like a bit of historical embroidery, there's no reason we here in the old country can't enjoy our own version of this classic. The crabcakes, well, they always bring to mind my own personal voyage of discovery. When I was working in the USA, I happened to be right on the doorstep of possibly the world's most famous seafood area, Chesapeake Bay. Every bar, every crabshack, every restaurant in the vicinity had its own version of crabcakes. This is ours. Serve it with the chowder and chargrilled corn to garnish. It's a combination as American as the fourth of July. **RS**

INGREDIENTS

For the crabcakes
500g white pasteurised crab meat
25g mayonnaise
1 egg
1 dessertspoon old bay seasoning
1 tbsp Dijon mustard
2 tsp Hendersons relish
Juice of ½ lemon
Small bunch of freshly chopped coriander
75g white breadcrumbs
1 chargrilled corn on the cob

For the sweetcorn chowder
2 corn on the cob
1 medium onion finely diced
2 sticks celery, diced into medium-sized chunks
1 large sweet potato peeled and diced into medium-sized chunks
2 cloves garlic, crushed
1 small glass white wine
125g butter
50g plain flour
2 tsp old bay seasoning
1 litre milk
3 finely-shredded spring onions
Salt and pepper
Chopped flat leaf parsley

For the chargrilled corn on the cob
4 corn on the cob
1 tbsp olive oil for brushing
Salt and pepper

METHOD

Crabcakes
1. Pick through the crab meat, ensuring there are no pieces of shell.
2. Beat the egg and lightly mix together with the old bay spice, mustard, Hendersons relish, mayonnaise, lemon juice and chopped coriander. (Leave to rest for 30 mins)
3. When everything is nicely mixed together add the breadcrumbs.
4. Form the crab cakes into a pastry cutter and refrigerate.
5. In a non-stick pan heat a little vegetable oil and add the crabcakes, lightly browning on each side
6. Place the cakes in a medium oven and bake for about 5 minutes. They are now ready to serve.

Sweetcorn chowder
1. In a non-stick frying pan heat a little vegetable oil and fry the corn on the cob until nicely browned all over.
2. Drain on kitchen paper. When cool enough to handle, remove all the sweetcorn kernels from the husk with a cook's knife and reserve.
3. In a saucepan, melt the butter and fry the onion and celery gently without colouring. Cook for a few minutes until softened.
4. Add the sweet potato and garlic and cook out for a minute.
5. Add the flour and stir with a wooden spoon until a roux is formed.
6. Cook over a low heat for a couple of minutes without colouring and add the wine, stirring constantly with a wooden spoon to prevent any lumps forming.
7. Now add the milk, old bay seasoning, salt and pepper and bring to the boil, then reduce to a simmer. Cook gently until the sweet potato is tender.
8. Add the sweetcorn kernels. Cook for a minute, add spring onions and chopped flat parsley.

Chargilled corn on the cob
1. Cut the corn into 4 pieces lengthways.
2. Brush the corn with the olive oil and season.
3. Heat the chargrill pan. Add the corn and brown all over. Place the corn into a medium oven and cook for 5 minutes.

TO SERVE

Heat the sweet corn chowder. Ladle into a deep plate. Place the crab cakes on top. Place a piece of chargrilled corn on top. Garnish with a sprig of flat parsley and serve.

CHEF'S TIPS

Go easy when binding the crabmeat into the mixture. It's a delicate meat, so don't overwork it or you'll spoil the texture. But above all, check for shell – there's nothing worse than biting into a piece. Have a taste of the mixture as you go along and adjust if necessary. Finally, fry a trial crabcake as a test before committing the whole batch to the pan. **RS**

RECOMMENDED WINES

3

California Chardoney

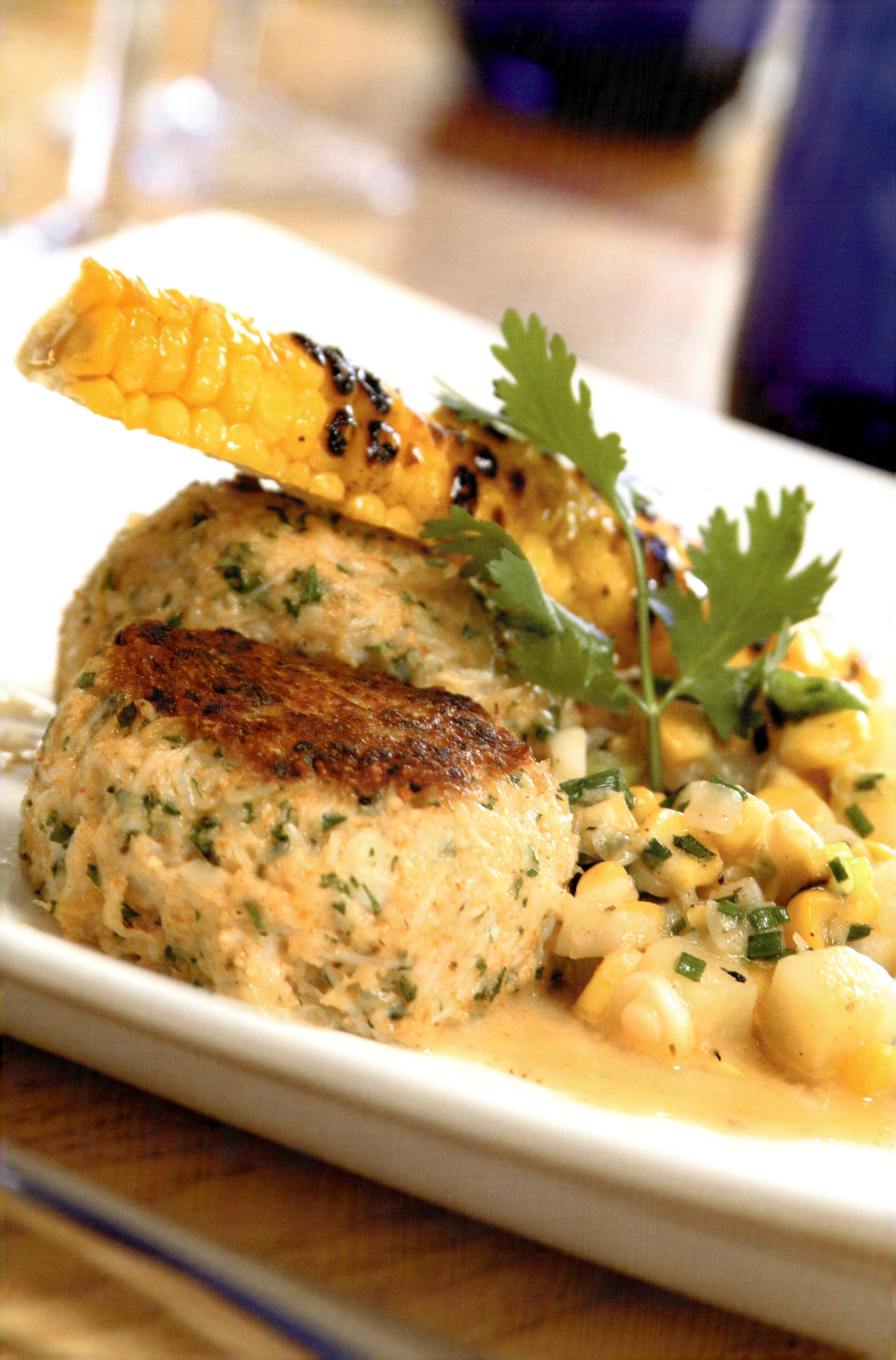

CLASSICS

SPAGHETTI BOLOGNESE

Before you wonder what a student staple is doing in a cookbook, let me assure you that this version is a world away from the 'fried mince with tomato puree' version. Rather than taking its cue from the great unwashed, this recipe was given to me by food writer Diane Seed, based in Rome. It's not a recipe that's set in stone; some people like to use just beef, but add it together with pancetta, the pork and sausages and you end up with a lovely, complex flavour. Before meeting Diane I'd never have dreamed of adding cream to finish the sauce, but believe me, it makes all the difference and helps the sauce cling to the pasta. **AC**

INGREDIENTS

100ml olive oil
100g pancetta, cubed
500g minced beef
500g minced pork
200g Italian sausages (out of their skins)
1 onion, diced (approx. 200g)
1 celery stick, diced (80g)
1 carrot, diced (100g)
4 large garlic cloves, chopped
Large glass white wine (175ml)
175ml brown stock
50g tomato purée
100ml double cream
1 x 500g pack dried De Cecco spaghetti
Fresh basil, chopped (optional)
Grated parmesan to serve

METHOD

1 Sweat the pancetta in olive oil until well coloured.
2 Add the onion, celery, carrot and garlic, and cook out without colouring for around 5 minutes.
3 Add the pork, beef mince and Italian sausages. Sweat down for 10 minutes, stirring with a wooden spoon until the meat has a little colour and stops clumping together.
4 Add the tomato purée, stock and white wine and cook slowly for around 1½ hours.
5 Add the cream, season with salt and pepper and cook out for 5 minutes.
6 Add the chopped basil.
7 Cook the spaghetti in plenty of boiling salted water to the packet instructions.
8 When cooked, drain and toss in with the Bolognese mix, reserving some sauce to put on top as extra.
9 Serve in large pasta bowls with plenty of grated parmesan.

CHEF'S TIPS

Contrary to foodie opinion, it's actually fine to use a standard cube to make the stock. Sweating away in the kitchen for a day and a half in an attempt to make the perfect home-made version – well, it's really not practical, nor is it worth the hassle. If you don't fancy the idea of using a packet version, most supermarkets handily carry a range of fresh stocks, which is a slightly better option. Make sure to use only lean beef and pork mince, as otherwise you'll end up with a large pool of discarded fat within the Bolognese sauce. **RS**

RECOMMENDED WINES

6 7
Punters Corner Cab Merlot/Barolo

THYME AFTER THYME

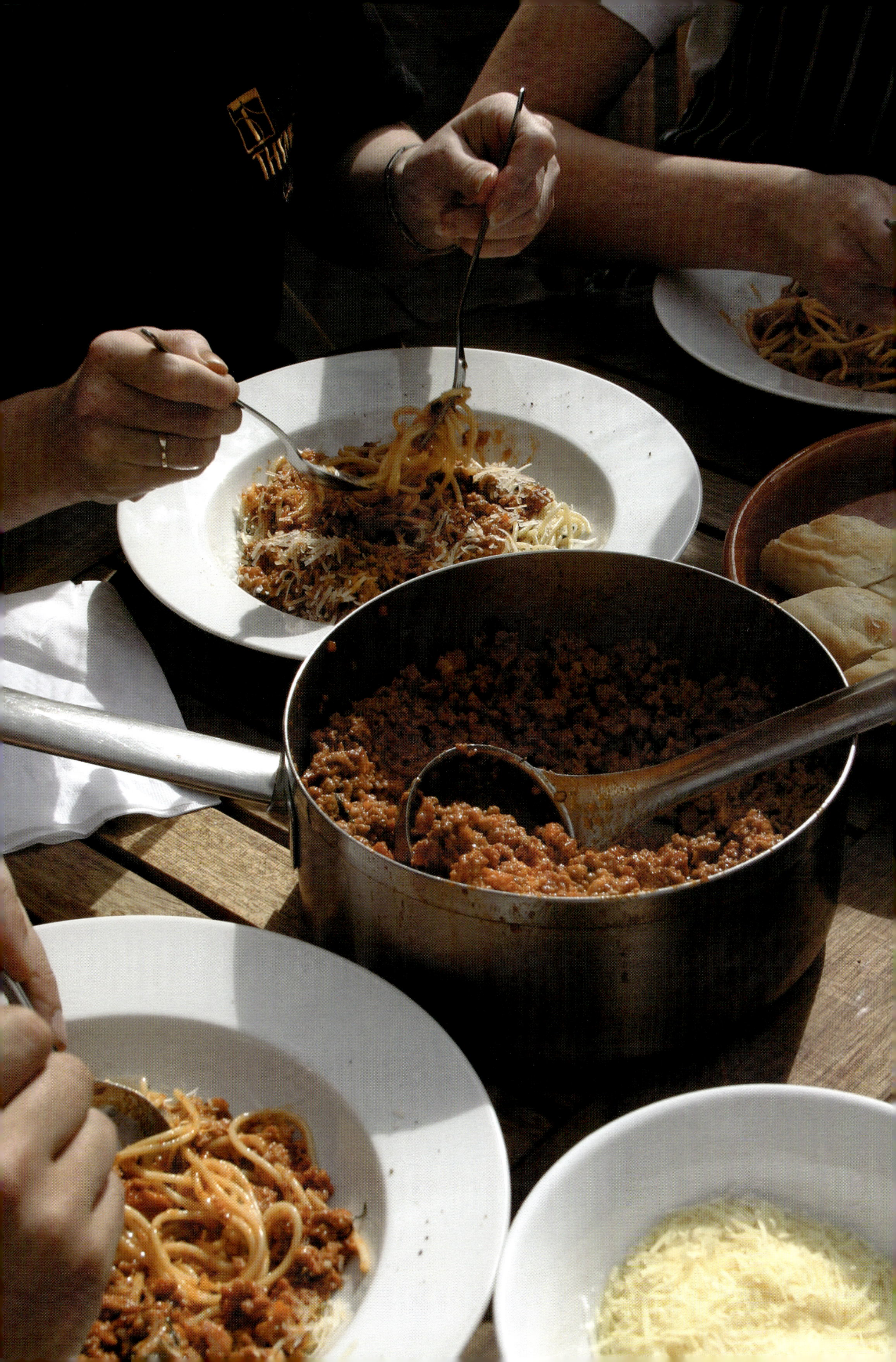

CHAPTER 3
A WORLD OF FLAVOURS

WORLD OF FLAVOURS

THAI-STYLE CHICKEN
udon noodle bowl

Wherever you travel in the country, you really can't avoid them. Noodles are the 'in thing' in food at the moment, and noodle bars are cropping up all over the place. They are as quintessentially oriental as pasta is Italian, and the idea can be traced right back to Marco Polo, who first brought noodles into the western consciousness by importing them from China in to Italy. At its essence, this dish is noodles and broth with a dressing, and it typifies the western take on cooking eastern cuisine. As far as oriental restaurants go, the king of them all has to be Nobu in London. However, lots of other less elevated establishments like Wagamamma's, one of the better chains, do dishes like this one really well. **RS**

INGREDIENTS

1 medium fresh chicken
3.5 litres water
1 large onion – diced
6 garlic cloves, crushed
50g fresh ginger, grated
2 large red chillis, chopped
125ml Thai fish sauce
100ml fresh lime juice
1 stick lemon grass, chopped
8 lime leaves, chopped
2 x 400ml can coconut milk
4 200g packets of udon noodles
2 limes, halved

Garnish
1 large carrot, julienned (thin strips)
20 mangetout
2 spring onions, shredded
1 red chilli, finely sliced
2 heads Pak Choi – washed and picked
80g beansprouts
8 pieces pickled ginger
100g toasted cashew nuts
20g black sesame seeds
Freshly-picked coriander leaves

METHOD

1 Cover the whole chicken with water and bring to the boil, reducing to a simmer.
2 Cook for around 1 hour, removing any scum from the pan as it is rises to the top.
3 Remove the chicken from the pan and strain the stock, reserving it for later.
4 Strip the chicken from the bone, discarding the skin and carcass.
5 In a large saucepan, sweat the onion without colouring and add the garlic and ginger.
6 Cook out for a minute and add the chilli, lemon grass and lime leaves.
7 Cook for another minute, then add the fish sauce, lime juice and chicken stock.
8 Bring to the boil, and reduce to a simmer.
9 Cook for about 40 minutes, and you'll end up with a lovely, fragrant stock.
10 Add the coconut milk, bring to the boil, and pass through a sieve.
11 Blanch the udon noodles. Blanch and refresh the carrots and mangetout.

TO SERVE

1 Place the warm udon noodles in the bottom of a large bowl, and top with the blanched carrots and mangetout.
2 Heat the broth in a saucepan and add the chicken.
3 When the chicken has heated through, add the Pak Choi leaves and wilt down.
4 Pour the stock, chicken and Pak Choi over the noodles.
5 Top with beansprouts, chilli, spring onions, pickled ginger, toasted cashews, sesame seeds and coriander leaves.
6 Garnish each dish with half a fresh lime. Serve immediately.

CHEF'S TIPS

In attempting any of the recipes in this book, it's a mantra worth repeating to yourself: preparation is all. Do everything beforehand, meticulously, and the cooking will be done in a flash. Prepare each ingredient, put it in a separate bowl and line each of them up ready to throw in to the mix. Repeatedly wipe down your chopping board and knife, so that everything is clean and ready to be cooked. **AC**

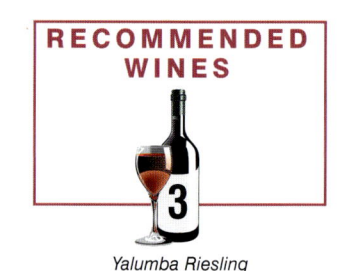

RECOMMENDED WINES

3

Yalumba Riesling

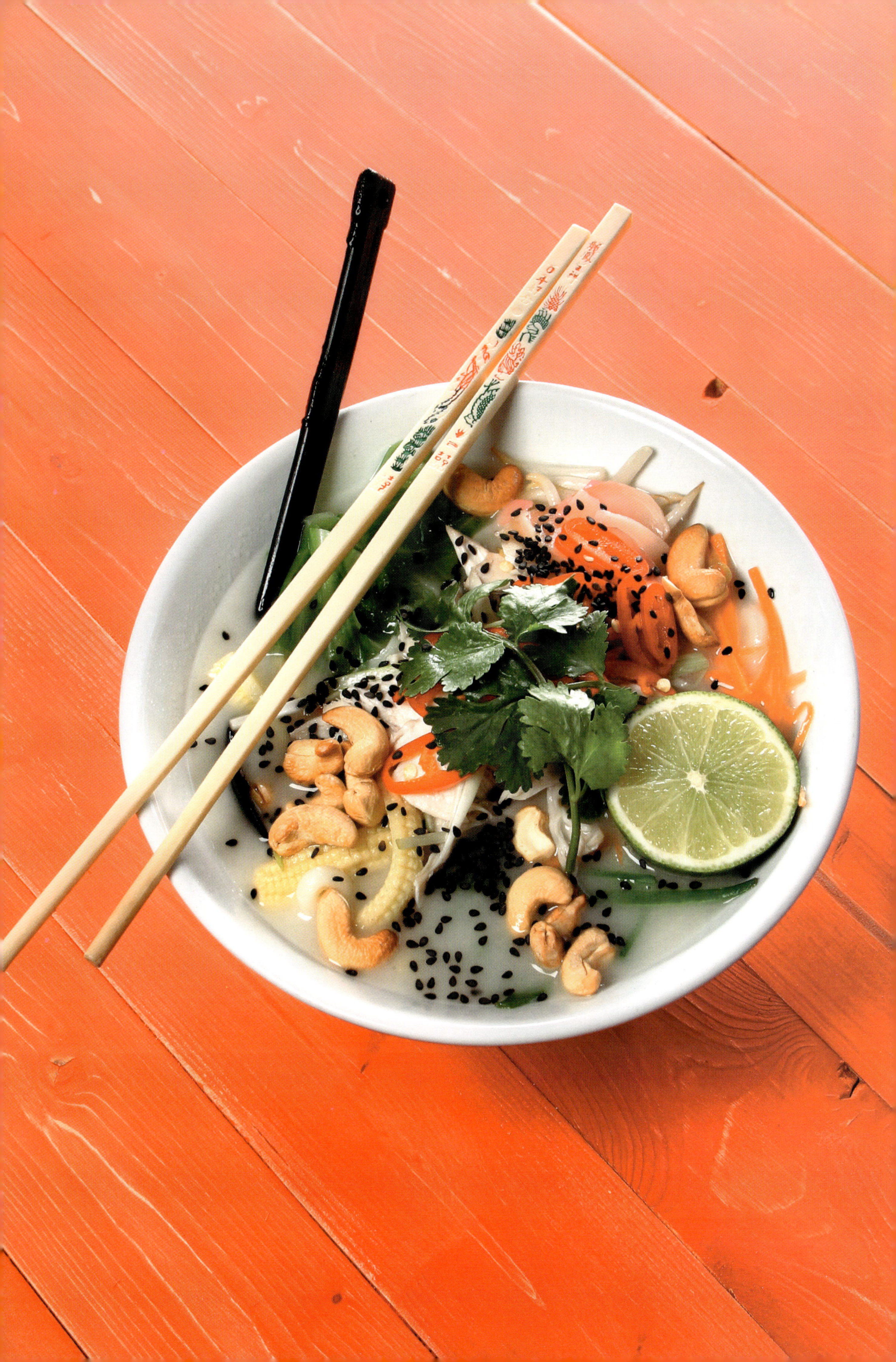

WORLD OF FLAVOURS

DUCK
and oriental vegetable spring rolls

There's no point in denying it. Yes, I'll hold up my hands and admit it – this is a version of that oriental restaurant staple, crispy duck pancakes. Except in this case, we've done them inside out. The pancakes are the crispy part, with the tender duck inside. This may sound a little strange, but it makes sense when you think about it. The addition of vegetables in the spring rolls makes the mixture within nice and moist. While we tend to regard duck as being fatty, but this is generally down to the skin; without its exterior, the meat is often dry, and needs the vegetables to create moisture. These eat really well with sweet chilli sauce, and the varieties you can buy in the supermarkets are excellent. **RS**

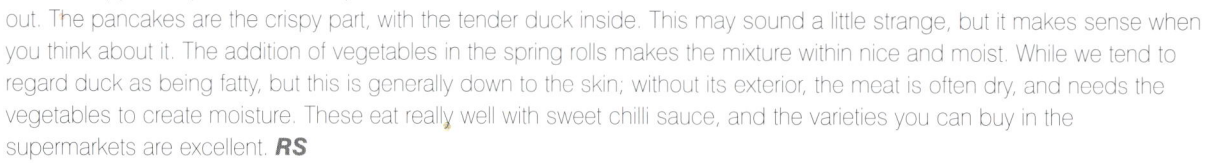

INGREDIENTS

½ shredded crispy duck
2 large carrots, julienned
2 large leeks, julienned
100g mangetout, julienned
200g beansprouts
10 baby sweetcorn, shredded
2 red peppers, shredded
4 heads Pak Choi, shredded
3 cloves garlic, crushed
50g pickled ginger, chopped
50ml sesame oil
1 red chilli, finely diced
25ml Japanese soy sauce
Bunch coriander, chopped
12 spring roll wrappers
1 egg, beaten

METHOD

1. Pick the duck from the carcass and shred.
2. Thinly slice all the vegetables and keep separately.
3. Mix together the crushed garlic, chilli, ginger, soy sauce and sesame oil.
4. Heat a thick-bottomed pan and fry the vegetables in a little oil until soft.
5. Add 1 tbsp of the garlic and chilli mixture to each vegetable for the final minute of frying – you will need to fry each veg seperately as they have different cooking times. Ensure each one is crisp, yet cooked inside.
6. Place all the vegetables on a large roasting tray to cool down.
7. Sprinkle generously with chopped coriander and add the shredded duck, mixing together well so everything is evenly distributed.
8. Pre-heat the fryer to 180°c.
9. Lay out the spring roll wrappers – do not let them dry out.
10. Place 2 tbsp of the filling in your hand and form into a cylinder shape.
11. Place on the wrapper, about a quarter of the way up.
12. Apply an egg wash around the outside of the wrapper, fold each side in and roll tightly, so the filling is completely and firmly enclosed.
13. Place in the fryer until golden, drain on kitchen paper and serve.

CHEF'S TIPS

Don't let the filling get too loose, as the results can make all your efforts amount to nothing. It really is especially important to wrap those spring rolls tightly, and avoid air bubbles as far as you can. They let oil leak in, and the result is greasy and unpleasant. As for the duck, it's actually much easier, and time-effective, to buy crispy duck ready-done from a supermarket. Or, if you have duck leg confit, this makes an excellent alternative. Remember you can fold the rolls into a variety of shapes (see photo above). **AC**

RECOMMENDED WINES

5

Cloudy Bay Pinot Noir (NZ)

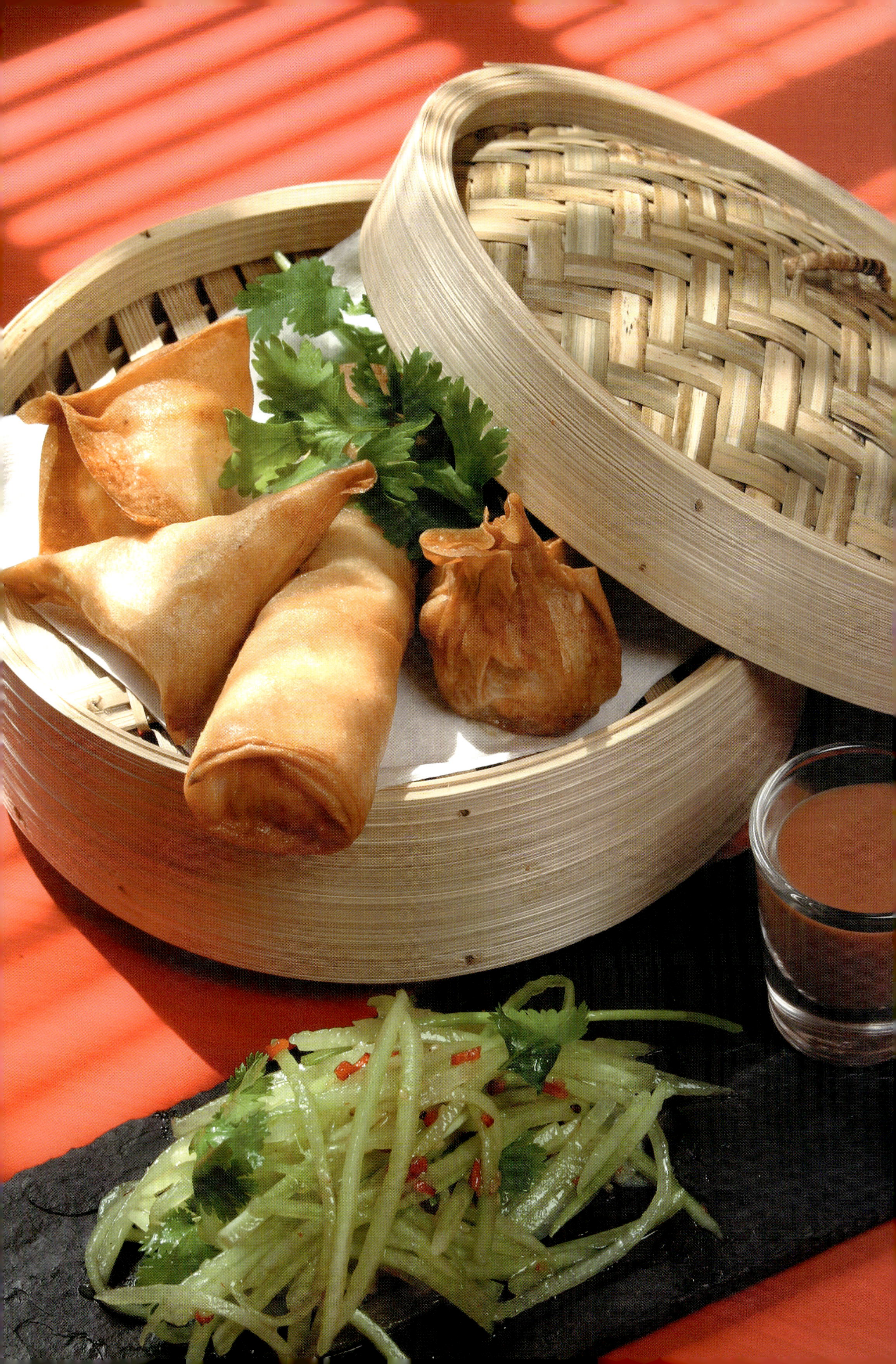

WORLD OF FLAVOURS

HOT AND SOUR SOUP
with seafood

Wherever you are in the world, you're likely to find an establishment serving up some sort of fish soup. In America it's known as chowder, while in France it's *soupe de poisson* – and you can hardly eat in an oriental restaurant and not have it as a starter. In fact, there's probably a rule against that kind of behaviour. In this version, the broth is the all-important factor. It should be a blend of hot and sour, and good enough for you to polish off on your own. You can buy ready-made wontons for steaming in oriental grocers, and these make the soup look especially good. For a slightly different taste, you can also add chicken or duck as well as, or instead of, the seafood. A vegetarian version works just as well – just tailor the soup to your own liking. **AC**

INGREDIENTS

1 batch chicken stock (see Extra Thyme)
1 lemon grass stick, finely chopped
8 lime leaves
50g fresh ginger, grated
125ml Thai fish sauce
4 shallots, thinly sliced
4 large garlic cloves, crushed
1 ½ red chillies, chopped
150ml fresh lime juice
4/5 whole star anise
8 tiger prawns
4 scallops
100g picked white crab meat
12 whole washed mussels, in the shell

Vegetable garnish
8 whole Pak Choi leaves
4 spring onions, shredded
1 carrot, julienned and blanched
8 mangetout, julienned & blanched
60g beansprouts
1 fresh chilli, finely sliced
8 pieces pickled ginger
freshly picked coriander leaves

METHOD

1 Sweat the shallots with the garlic and ginger.
2 Add the chilli, lemon grass, lime leaves, chicken stock, fish sauce, lime juice and star anise.
3 Bring to the boil, reduce to a simmer and cook gently for 20 minutes.
4 Strain through a fine sieve and reserve.
5 The soup should be very fragrant, with a touch of heat and a slight sour note from the lime juice.
6 Adjust the flavours to your own preference by adding a little more lime or chilli, but remember that you are going to garnish with sliced chilli.

TO SERVE

1 In a large pan, bring the soup to the boil.
3 Add the prawns and mussels, and cook for 1 minute.
3 Add the mangetout, carrot, beansprouts and Pak Choi.
4 Pour evenly into large oriental soup bowls and add the picked crab, sliced chillis, pickled ginger and picked coriander.

CHEF'S TIPS

It may seem strange to use chicken as opposed to fish stock, but it gives the soup a better balance. Fish stock, as far as I'm concerned, just isn't strong enough for this soup. Try out different versions until you hit on a formula that works for you; if you're cooking for vegetarians, make up a miso-based soup from a little paste. Use whatever seafood is both good and available at the time; the ones recommended here are just suggestions. Whatever options you choose, don't go for too intense a chilli flavour, as it can easily overwhelm the dish. **RS**

RECOMMENDED WINES

3

Riesling

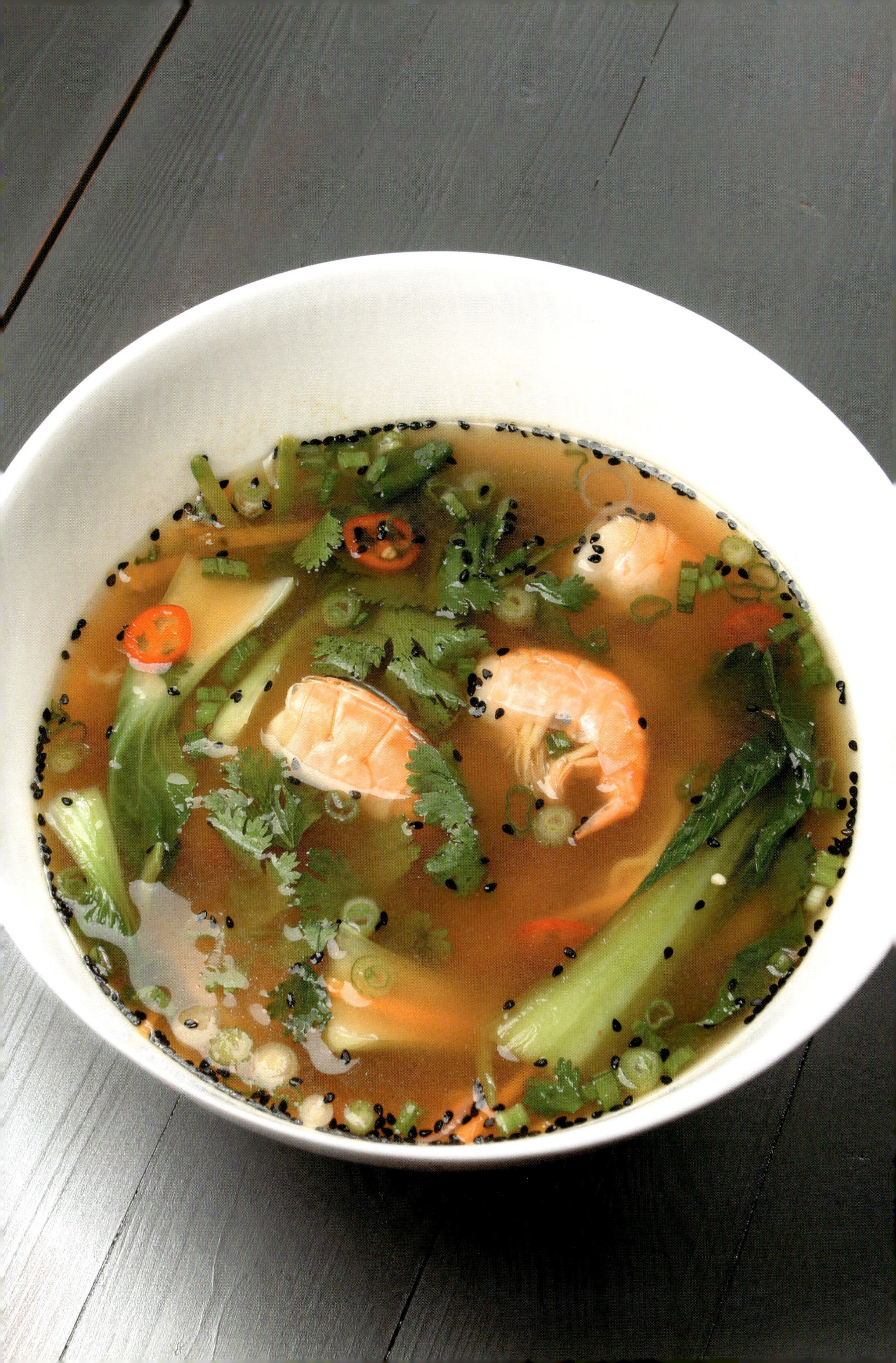

WORLD OF FLAVOURS

SALMON AND PRAWN CURRY

Along with fish and chips, curry is one of Britain's most popular take-out foods. Sadly, despite being a full-blown national dish, the curry struggles to shed its image of being only for the stomachs of those who've consumed copious amounts of lager beforehand. With many customers not always being in a position to cast a careful critical eye over what's being served up, curry has acquired a mass-produced image. However, that's beginning to change. Places like the Michelin-starred Cinnamon Club in London show that Indian cuisine can compare favourably with the very best. This particular dish will hopefully inspire you to have a go at making a curry for yourself. It's a bit more refined than the variety you'll find within darkly-lit establishments in the side streets of the city centre, but having said that, I wouldn't discourage you from enjoying it with a glass of Indian lager, or a drop of Gewurztraminer. **RS**

INGREDIENTS

500g fresh salmon fillet
300g cooked king prawns
2 tbsp vegetable oil
1 tsp mustard seeds
10 curry leaves
pinch fenugreek seeds
1 onion, finely diced
½ tsp turmeric
1 green chilli, finely diced
1 tsp ground coriander
1 tsp ground cumin
1 x 400g can chopped tomatoes
4 large garlic cloves, crushed
50g grated ginger
Salt
300g canned coconut milk
75g butter
Freshly chopped coriander

METHOD

1 Heat the vegetable oil in a large saucepan until it starts to smoke.
2 Add the curry leaves and fry for 1 minute.
3 Add the mustard and fennel seeds, and fry for 30 seconds. Add the onions and sweat for 5 minutes.
4 Add the butter and wait until it starts to foam, before adding the garlic, chilli, ginger, ground coriander, cumin and turmeric.
5 Cook the spices for around 5 minutes, stirring from time to time.
6 Add the chopped tomatoes, and return to the boil.
7 Add the coconut milk, reduce to a simmer and cook for 10-15 minutes.
8 Cut the salmon fillet into large chunks, seal in a hot pan and add to the curry.
9 Cook for a couple of minutes, add the prawns, gently heat and stir in the chopped coriander.

TO SERVE

Spoon into bowls and serve with plain boiled rice and naan bread.

CHEF'S TIPS

This dish will cure the affliction known as 'curry powder-itis'. There's nothing like a curry made with your own seeds and spices; it's more satisfying, and not as intense. Curry powder, and paste, has a rawness that always suggests to me that it needs to be cooked more. Cook the salmon carefully, even to the point of under-cooking, and let the residual heat finish it off for you. This should help you obtain the desired result of chunks of salmon that will give the dish a pleasant texture. Otherwise, the flakes just disappear into the sauce, in which case the salmon may as well not be in there at all. **AC**

RECOMMENDED WINES

Alsace Gewurztraminer

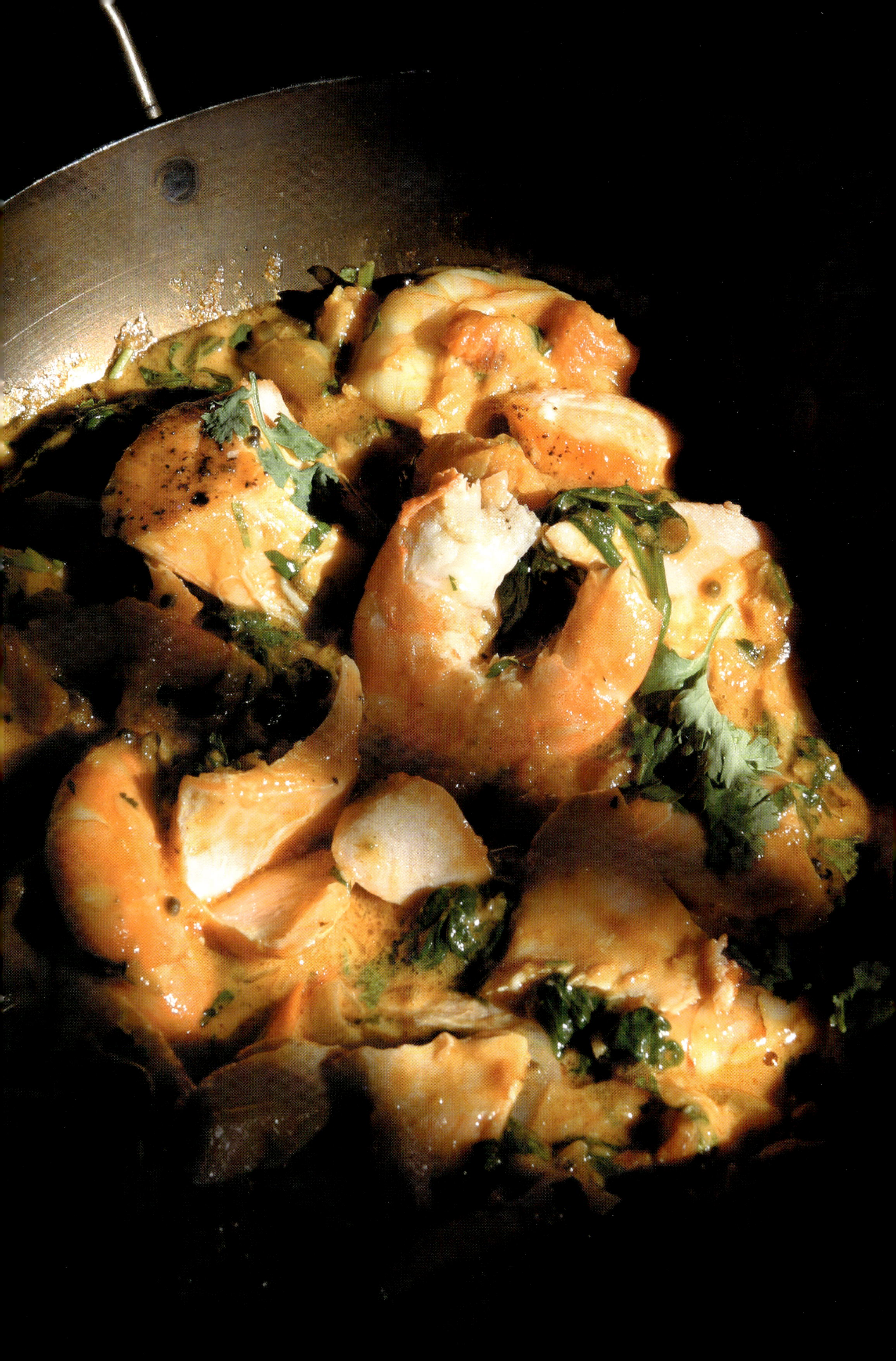

WORLD OF FLAVOURS

BANG BANG CHICKEN
with vegetable salad

This dish is unique in the book in that it has its origins in Malaysia. It's a version of satay, which I actually first tried out in America many moons ago. I was working for Sir Bernard Ashley, the co-founder of the Laura Ashley chain, who had a hotel in Virginia. I sampled the dish at a local oriental restaurant on one of our numerous excursions; the Ashleys used to encourage us to eat out as much as possible. There are many people who think of America and its restaurants only in terms of the mass and volume of the food on the plate. But I've eaten at what I consider to be some of the best restaurants in the world in the US. For example, The French Laundry in Napa Valley, or Charlie Trotter's in Chicago, and the Gramercy Tavern and many others in New York. The trick to good food, wherever in the world you happen to be, is inspiration. I'm sending our head chef down to London soon to try out a number of restaurants, not all of them grand and fine, and I hope he comes back with the sort of renewed enthusiasm that will be reflected in fresh influences on Thyme's menu. This dish is a good example of the sort of unusual item that jumps off the menu, saying 'eat me', and that's the effect we're trying to replicate. **RS**

INGREDIENTS
4 skinless chicken breasts
1 jar crunchy peanut butter
350ml sweet chilli sauce
4 heads baby gem lettuce
½ cucumber, deseeded and sliced
60g beansprouts
1 large carrot, julienned
80g French beans, blanched
150ml lime and sesame dressing (see Extra Thyme)
Bunch picked coriander leaves
2 limes

METHOD
1 Pre-heat oven to 200°c.
2 Season and seal the chicken breasts in a hot pan, and place into the oven at for 10 minutes.
3 Heat the crunchy peanut butter in the microwave (this makes it easier to work with), mix together with the sweet chilli sauce and reserve.
4 Wash and drain the salad leaves and beansprouts, and pat dry.
5 Cut all the vegetables, leaves and beansprouts and toss together with the sesame and lime dressing.
6 Spread each cooked chicken breast with the peanut mixture and place under the grill until melted.

TO SERVE
Arrange the salad mixture equally between 4 plates. Top with the glazed chicken breasts and garnish with picked coriander.

CHEF'S TIPS
It may sound exotic, but really this dish is simplicity in itself. I'm not being facetious when I say that if you can open an oven door, you can cook it. The only pitfall is in the balance of the sauce: the lime juice and fish sauce are quite sharp, and while this is fine if you enjoy this kind of flavour it may prove to be a little excessive for those who don't. So, make sure to adjust the balance of the dressing before serving it with the dish. **AC**

RECOMMENDED WINES

Kim Crawford NZ Sauvignon Blanc

enjoy food & drink

WORLD OF FLAVOUR

THAI PRAWN CAKES

Along with crème brulée, this would be one of my desert island dishes. It was one of the first things I did at my own restaurant, and the accompaniments haven't changed either: sweet potato crisps and peanut pesto work really well with it. It's particularly in vogue right now, what with Thai cooking being so popular at present. This is a simple dish to make, and is always guaranteed to impress friends. Originally, it started off as a result of our kitchen's humorous 'Mr Saturday night' menu options. In other words, we'd do something with prawns, something with steak and something with chocolate. This, after all, is a variation on a prawn dish. I ended up having to take it off the menu because it sold so many. Seven out of every 10 people would have this as a starter, and I got bored of peeling prawns! The consistency and style varies according to who makes it. In fact, the authentic Thai version is quite rubbery, and not so attractive to the western palate. **RS**

INGREDIENTS

1kg peeled black tiger prawns
½ red chilli, finely chopped
25g pickled ginger, chopped
6 lime leaves, chopped
1 stick lemon grass, chopped
25g fresh coriander, chopped
5g mint, chopped
5g black sesame seeds
8g green chilli, chopped
2 dessertspoons of sesame oil
25g Thai fish sauce
1 garlic clove, crushed
Peanut pesto (see Extra Thyme)

METHOD

1 Pre-heat oven to 180°c.
2 Place half the prawns into a food processor, along with all the other ingredients.
3 Pulse until everything is mixed together.
4 Add the remainder of the prawns to the mix and pulse gently, taking care that the prawns are not broken down too much.
5 Form into 100g cakes and shallow-fry for 1 minute on each side.
6 Place in the oven for 3-4 minutes, and serve.

TO SERVE

Serve 2 cakes per person, along with peanut pesto, dressed leaves, and sweet potato crisps.

CHEF'S TIPS

Keeping it simple here will pay dividends. It may cost you a bit more, but only use prawns – don't be tempted to bulk out the cakes with fish. To get things perfect, always fry one cake first as a sampler. Nine times out of 10 you'll need to adjust it in some way, and testing one out initially will save you a lot of heartache. It may well need a touch more spiciness, or a little more fragrance. If this is the case, just use the ginger, garlic, lime leaves or chilli as appropriate. **AC**

RECOMMENDED WINES

4

Punters Corner Chardonnay –
oaked, big chardonnay

THYME AFTER THYME

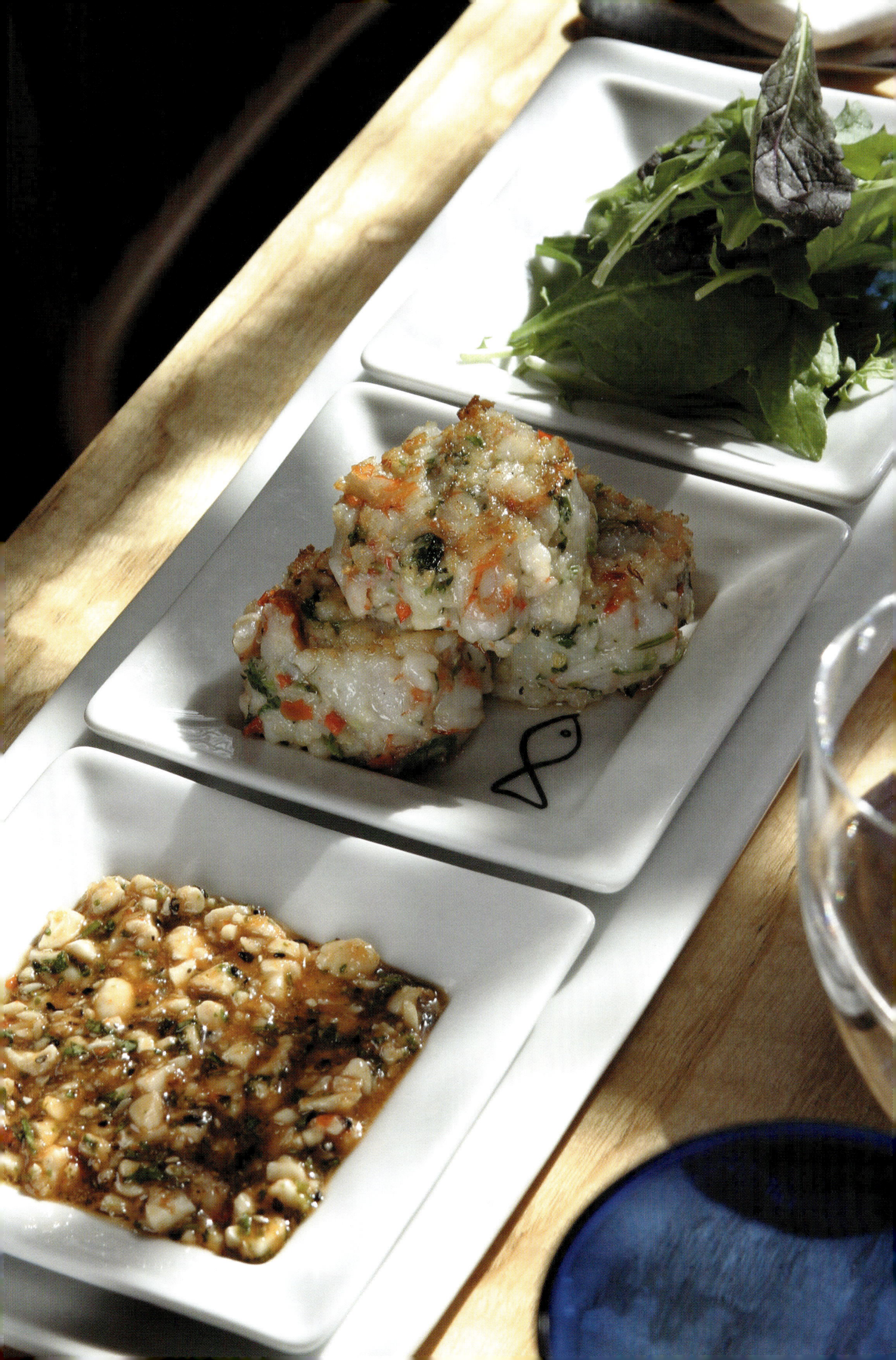

WORLD OF FLAVOURS

RIBEYE STEAK
with teryaki sauce, sweet potato tempura and pak choy

Ladies and gentlemen, I give you steak, chips and gravy, eastern-style. You'll love these flavours. And yes, I've chosen this particular cut of meat for a reason. Get a good ribeye and it'll be the best steak you've ever had. The tenderness is unsurpassed. As for the accompaniments, there's the lovely stickiness of the teriyaki sauce that helps it cling to the meat. The pak choy – which the Americans seemed to be using in everything when I was last over there – completes the eastern theme nicely. Go on, have a go at this. **RS**

INGREDIENTS
4 x 250g extra mature ribeye steaks
Salt and pepper
200g japanese soy sauce
75g mirin
50g sake
100g sugar
15g cornflour
35ml water to mix cornflour
Sweet potato tempura and pak choy (see Extra Thyme)

METHOD
1. Add the sake to a small saucepan and stir over a medium heat for 1 minute to cook out the alcohol.
2. Add the mirin, soy and sugar and bring to the boil.
3. Mix the cornflour and water into a paste and add to the sauce to thicken slightly.
4. Reserve.
5. Season the steaks with salt and pepper.
6. Seal in a hot frying pan on each side.
7. Place the frying pan in the oven and cook to your liking.

TO SERVE
Place the steaks on the plates and pour over the teryaki sauce. Serve with pak choy & sweet potato tempura.

CHEF'S TIPS
Ask your butcher for extra-mature ribeye steaks. We specify these at Thyme Café and we never have a complaint about tough steak. And don't be tempted to take the lazy way out by nipping down to the shops for a bottle of commercially-made teriyaki sauce. It's worth making your own. Why not make a large batch while you're at it and keep the rest for future use – it'll be usable for a couple of weeks if kept in a sealed container in the fridge. **AC**

RECOMMENDED WINES

Claret/Big Pinotage/Cabernet

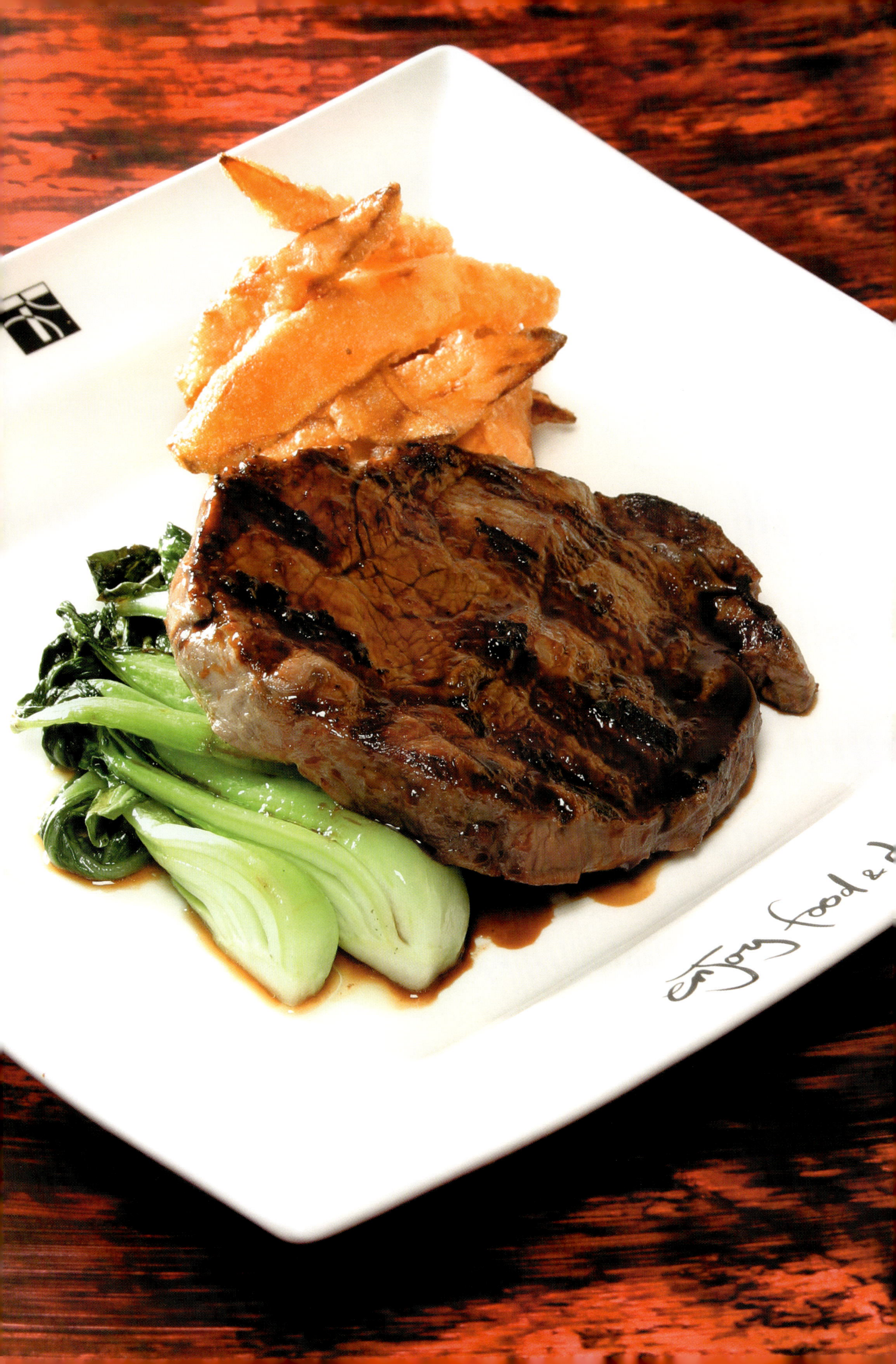
enjoy food &

WORLD OF FLAVOURS

SALMON MISO
with soba noodle salad

I picked up the inspiration for this dish during my time in Japan. That was the start of my love affair with oriental cooking, which I carry on whenever time allows at possibly my favourite restaurant of all, Nobu in London. Their use of flavours and presentation is truly inspiring. But top-drawer stuff like that is only part of the story about Japanese food. At the other end of the scale, I have fond memories of the tempura bars you can see on almost every street. I suppose they're the equivalent of our chippies. Many was the time I'd tuck into some delightful crisp tempura with a big bowl of rice and the traditional accompaniment, a bottle of beer.

This particular dish takes a slightly more westernised theme, although it uses authentic ingredients. The mirin is a sweet cooking wine. Like the miso, a fermented soya bean paste, you can find it at most supermarkets. The soba noodles are made with buckwheat flour and again should be easy to get hold of. **AC**

INGREDIENTS

4 x 200 g salmon fillets
250 g light miso paste
100 g sugar
100 g mirin
100 g sake
600 g cooked soba noodles
4 spring onions finely shredded
½ cucumber, seeds removed and thinly sliced
Bunch coriander leaves
2 tsp black sesame seeds
200 ml soy–mirin dressing (see basics)
60 g pickled ginger, shredded

METHOD

1. Bring the sake to the boil, burning off the excess alcohol.
2. Add the mirin, miso paste and sugar, whisking until a smooth paste is formed.
3. Pour into a bowl and allow to cool.
4. When the mixture is completely cool dip the salmon in the mix.
5. Place in the fridge to marinate for 24 hours.
6. Cook the soba noodles to packet instructions, drain & refresh.
7. Toss with the cucumber, coriander, spring onion, pickled ginger, sesame seeds and soy-mirin dressing. Split evenly between 4 plates.
8. Heat a large frying pan with a little oil, then fry the marinated salmon for a couple of minutes on each side.
9. Place in the oven for 4–5 minutes.
10. The salmon should be nice and caramelised on the outside yet slightly rare on the inside.
11. Place the salmon on top of the noodles, drizzle a little soy-mirin dressing around the outside and serve.

CHEF'S TIPS

If this book achieves one thing above all, I hope it convinces readers that enjoying a different cooking experience is no harder than preparing a mundane meal. Once you've taken the trouble to source the ingredients, here's something that will add a little excitement to the midweek menu. And it's no more of a challenge than making a conventional pasta dish. If you really are so pushed for time that you believe you'll never fit this into your schedule (in which case, don't let the ministerial duties get too much on top of you) then you can marinate the salmon beforehand. It will, if necessary, keep for a couple of days in the fridge. When searing the salmon, use a medium heat and a non-stick pan with just a dash of oil. Wipe off the excess marinade before frying to ensure you get a nicely seared result. **AC**

RECOMMENDED WINES

Roaring Forties Tasmanian Pinot Noir

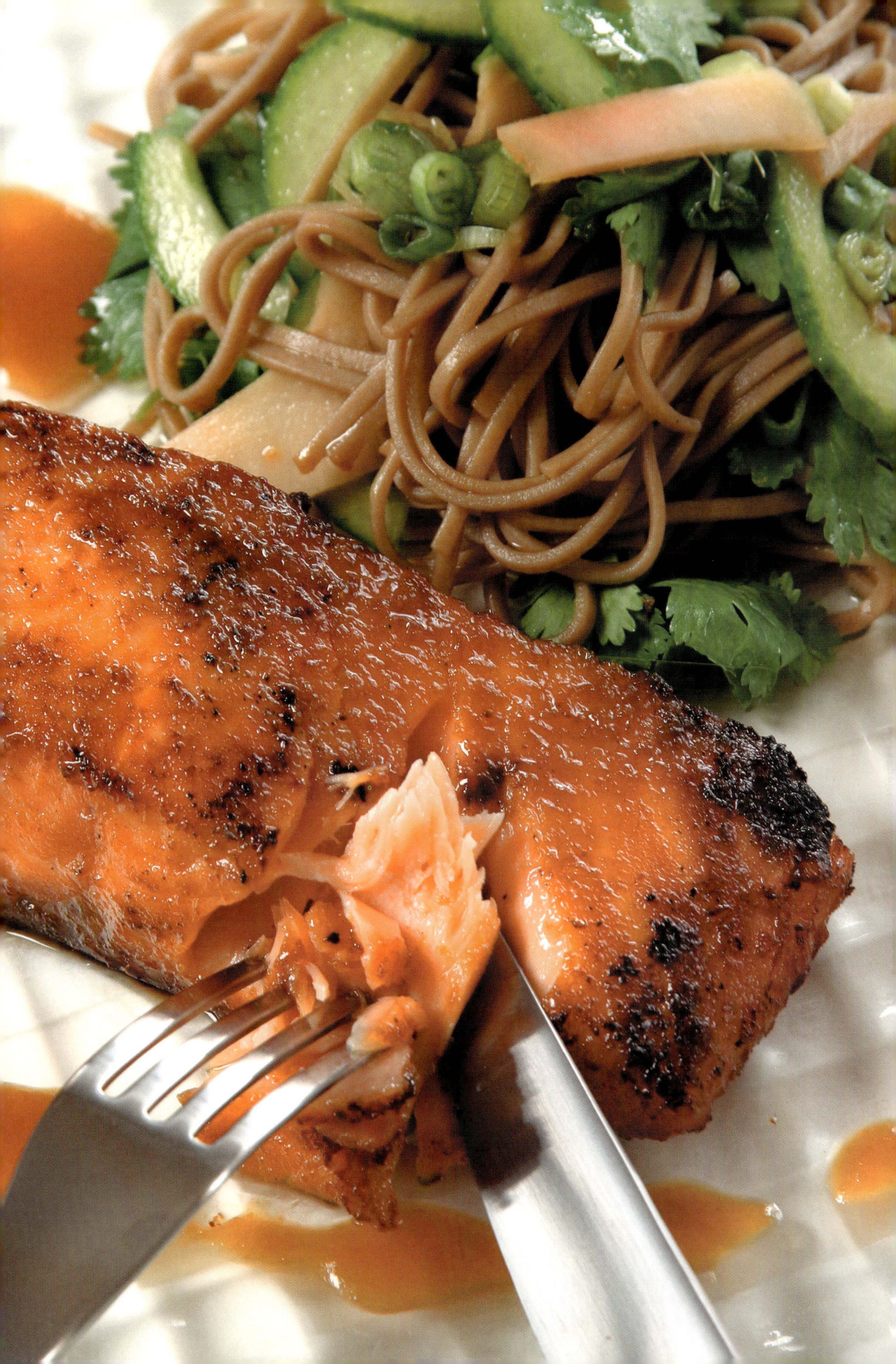

WORLD OF FLAVOURS

BRAISED TERYAKI MUSHROOMS

This is so easy to do, even my small son William couldn't go far wrong with it. Have it as a starter, or as a side accompaniment to steak or an oriental dish. It's modern, and surprisingly healthy. The field mushrooms are delightfully steaky in texture, and it's the kind of dish that sits well within a café-style venue. **RS**

INGREDIENTS
500g open cap field mushrooms
1 tbsp vegetable oil
150g Teryaki sauce (see Extra Thyme)
4 spring onion, finely shredded
50g pickled ginger, julienned

METHOD
1. Pre-heat oven to 200°c.
2. Heat the oil in a large frying pan.
3. Fry each side of the mushrooms until well sealed.
4. Place the mushrooms in an earthenware or ovenproof dish, and pour over the Teryaki sauce.
5. Place in the oven and bake for 10-15 minutes.
6. Five minutes before serving sprinkle the spring onions and ginger over the mushrooms.
7. Serve immediately.

CHEF'S TIPS
There's only one thing to really watch out for here, and that is in the fine shredding of the spring onion and the julienning of the pickled ginger. Look after those fingers; curl them in towards you, and hold the knife against the protruding knuckle. This way, you can cut away with impunity, and save the casualty department of your local hospital the trouble of a visit. **AC**

RECOMMENDED WINES

4

NZ Chardonnay

THYME AFTER THYME

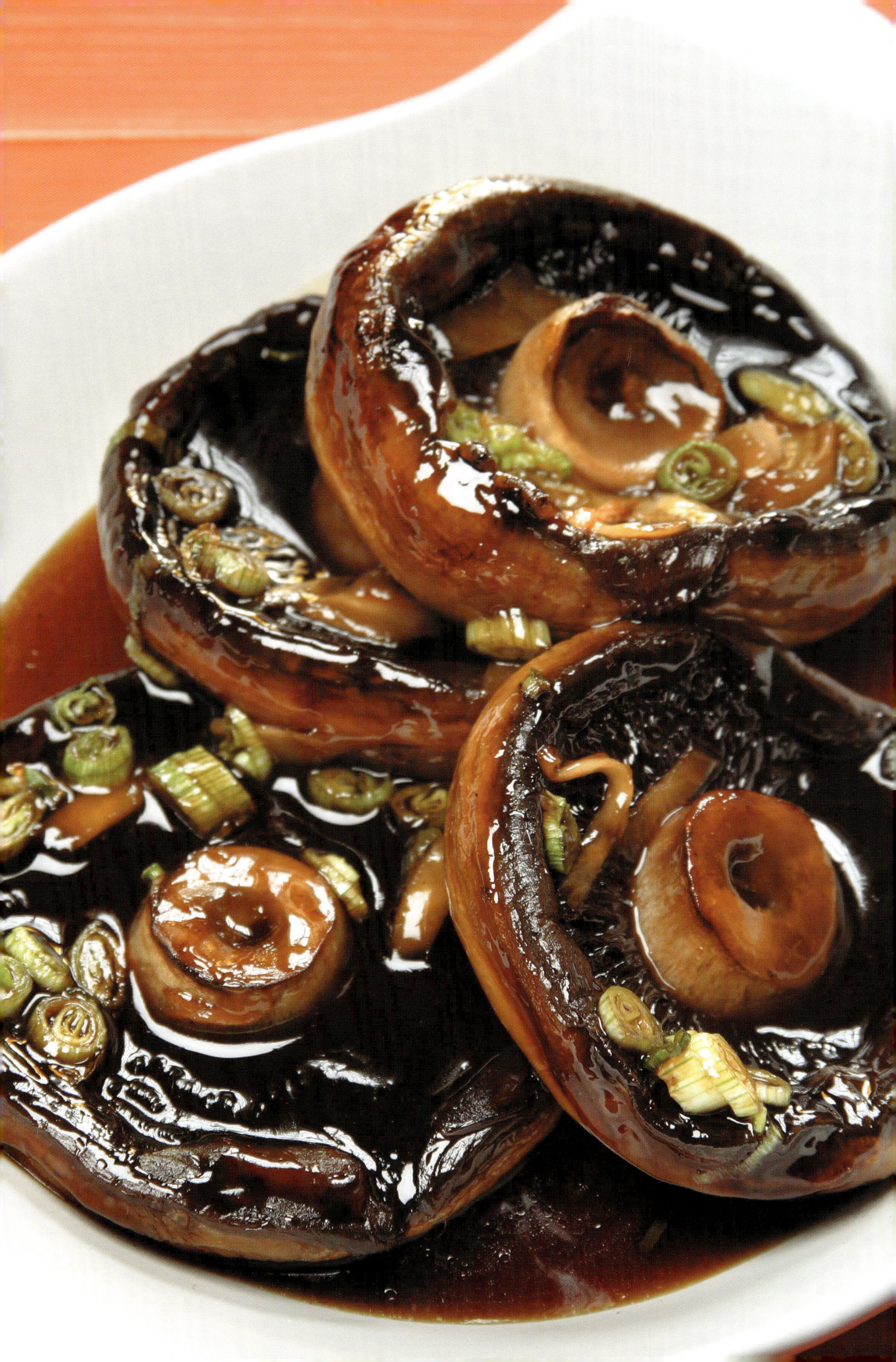

CHAPTER 4
DESSERTS

DESSERTS

BAKED CHOCOLATE PUDDING

It's a well-known fact that everyone loves chocolate, but this dish is especially decadent. There's a lovely contrast between the crispness of the pudding and the sticky, gooey fondant inside that demands further helpings. I first had this dish in New York 12 years ago with one of my heroes, the chef John-Georges Vongerichten. He's the owner of a number of restaurants over there, including Vong and Jo-Jo's, and I'm just glad I was introduced to such a great version of it. I suppose you could say that this dish has become the new black forest gateau – everyone has a recipe for it. It's one of the sort of enduringly popular dishes I always like to include on our menus. **RS**

INGREDIENTS

150g unsalted butter, melted
100g dark chocolate, melted
2 eggs
2 egg yolks
100g caster sugar
50g cocoa powder
75g plain flour

METHOD

1 Pre-heat oven to 190°c.
2 Sieve the flour and cocoa powder and reserve.
3 Melt the chocolate and the butter.
4 Whisk the eggs and sugar together in an electric mixer, until doubled in volume.
5 Gently fold in the flour and cocoa, followed by the chocolate and butter.
6 Grease the ramekins or aluminium moulds, and sprinkle with cocoa powder, shaking out the excess.
7 Pour in the chocolate mix and bake in the oven for 8-10 minutes.

TO SERVE

Turn out the cooked puddings onto a dessert plate and pour over a chocolate orange sauce (see Extra Thyme). This would eat particularly well with a scoop of vanilla ice cream, or if you prefer, a white chocolate ice cream.

CHEF'S TIPS

The essence of this is the quality of the chocolate. Use the very best you can afford; brands such as Callebaut, or, better still, Valrhona. Really push the boat out, as it makes all the difference. The other main issue is to get your timing right. Cook it through and you get a cake for afternoon tea – a consolation prize, of sorts – undercook it, and you've got chocolate sauce. The trick is to get a result somewhere in between, so that you cut into the pudding and the filling inside oozes out. To tell if you're there, insert a skewer. If it comes out clean, it's overcooked. If it oozes out slightly, and the top is just set, then you have the perfect pudding. Make an extra pudding or two, turn them out and see what they're like. A confident chef serves this by itself, but if you need an accompaniment go for ice cream or a mint or orange sorbet, which both provide a nice contrast in temperatures. **RS**

RECOMMENDED WINES

Antinori VIN Santo

THYME AFTER THYME

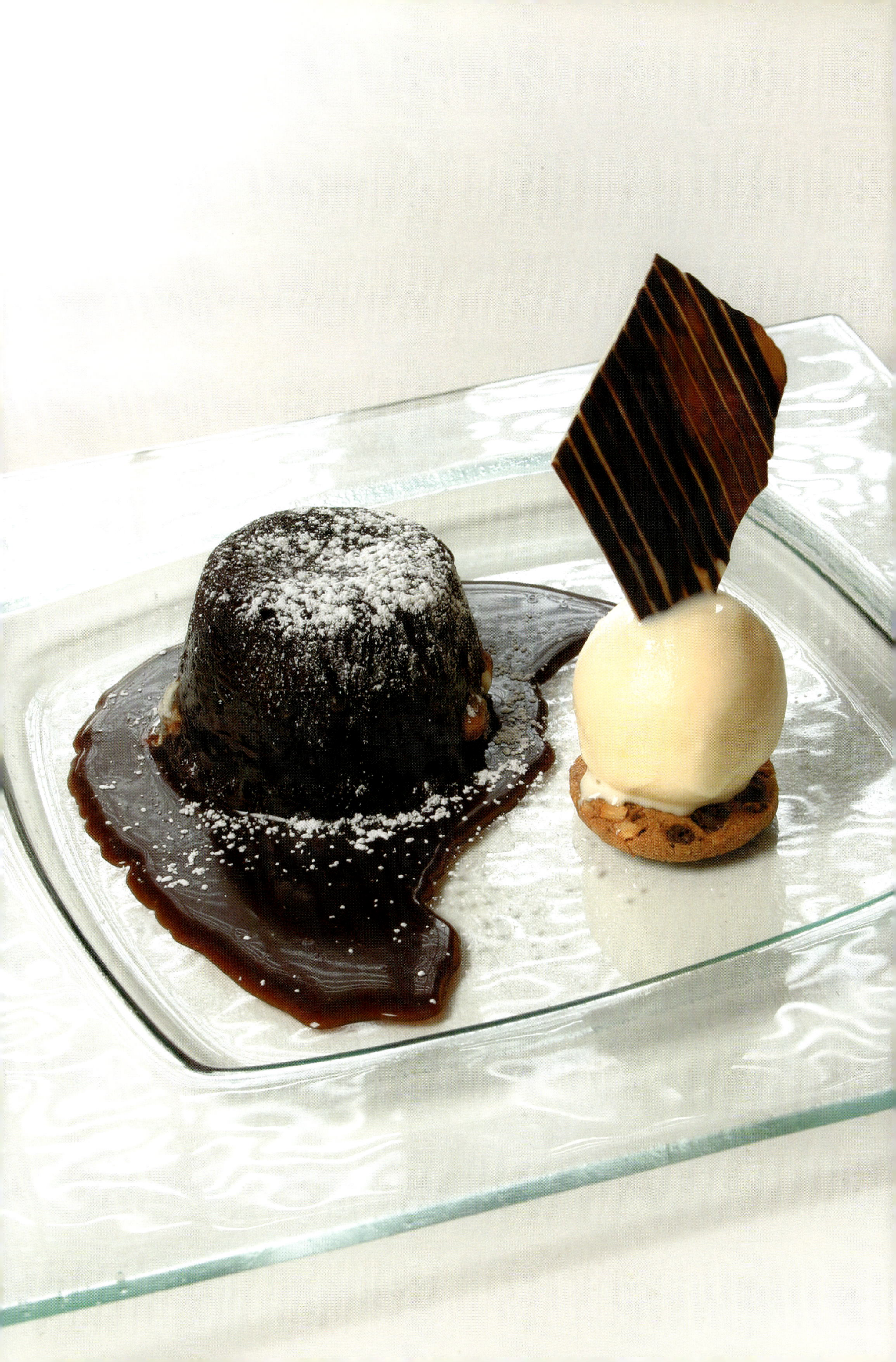

DESSERTS

BANANA AND BANOFFEE CRUMBLE

Everyone gets the idea that 'banoffee' is an American creation, but that's actually not correct. It was thought up in a restaurant in Sussex, when someone had the courage to stew a tin of condensed milk for four hours until the milk turned to toffee. Banana and toffee go together like strawberries and cream, or chocolate and mint. This principle is generally the basis on which we approach a menu; we look at what flavours work, and build a dish around it. **RS**

INGREDIENTS

200g plain flour
200g granary flour
200g unsalted butter
200g demerara sugar
4 large bananas
1 x 400g tin condensed milk
1 batch rum and raisin custard (see Extra Thyme)

METHOD

1. Pre-heat oven to 190°c.
2. In a saucepan, completely cover a tin of condensed milk with water and simmer gently for about 4 hours.
3. Allow to cool.
4. Rub the two flours and butter together, add the sugar, and rub until crumbed.
5. Peel and slice the bananas, and place in the base of the ovenproof ear dishes.
6. Open the can of condensed milk, which should form a lovely thick toffee, and split evenly between the 4 dishes.
7. Top generously with the crumble mixture and place in the oven for 10-12 minutes.
8. Serve immediately, along with rum and raisin custard.

CHEF'S TIPS

Put on those safety goggles, and hide your valuable crockery in a safe place. Unless you fancy redecorating your kitchen in a slightly haphazard way, remember that a tin of condensed milk can have an explosive force close to a small hand grenade, and keep the tin covered as you cook it for four hours. Ensure there's liquid in there and you'll be safe; don't, and you're in trouble. **RS**

RECOMMENDED WINES

8

Cordon Cut Riesling Mt Horrocks

THYME AFTER THYME

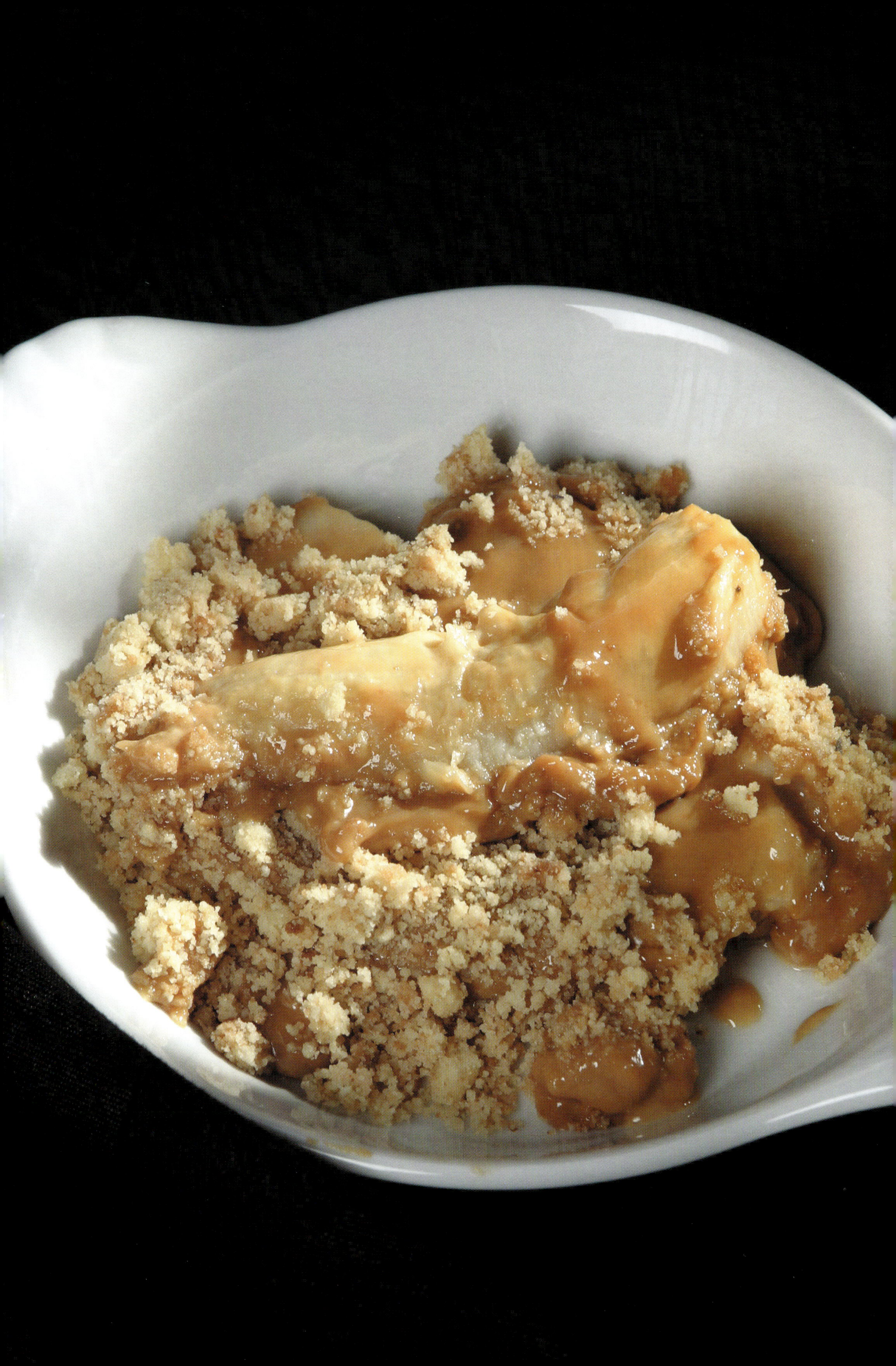

DESSERTS

WARM CHERRIES
with Mascarpone

Simple, easy to prepare and stunning to look at: that's how I'd describe this wonderful dish. It's one I only cook when the cherries are at their glorious best in June or July, and I've included it in the book for two reasons: one, I like it (a very important consideration), and two, fruit desserts are often served cold. Try this out as a warm dish and you won't regret it, I guarantee you. The mascarpone gives a rich, luxurious edge to the dish, but vanilla ice cream or fromage frais will also do the job. Likewise with the alcohol, you can alternatively use kirsch, champagne or amaretto. The dish's origins lie in that old school classic cherries jubilee, that was always flambéed at the customer's table. No such fuss here, thankfully. **RS**

INGREDIENTS
800g pitted cherries
200g caster sugar
2 lemons, juice only
100ml cherry brandy
Mascarpone cheese

METHOD
1 Stone the cherries.
3 Place half in a blender along with the brandy, lemon juice and sugar. Purée until smooth.
4 Heat the purée until hot (but not boiling), pour the hot cherry sauce over the remaining cherries and steep.

TO SERVE
Heat the cherries in a small pan. Serve simply in a bowl, along with a spoon of the Mascarpone cheese (or, if you prefer, this dish eats really well with vanilla ice cream).

CHEF'S TIPS
This dessert is simplicity itself. All you need look out for is the consistency of the compote. Don't let it get too watery (just cook it down a little longer if this is the case) and don't kill it by over-use of the alcohol. **AC**

RECOMMENDED WINES

Vin Santo Antinori

THYME AFTER THYME

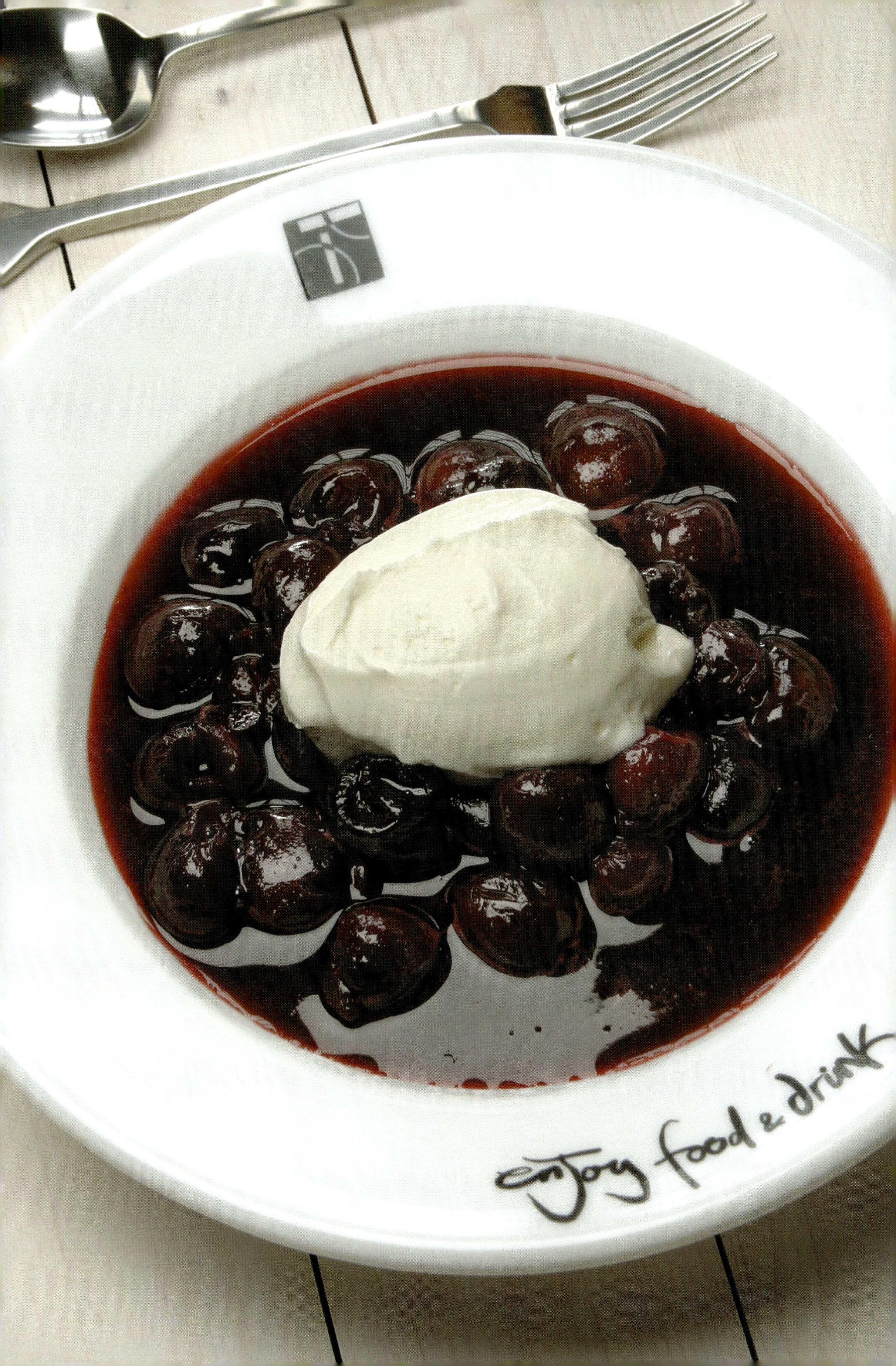
enjoy food & drink

DESSERTS

RASPBERRY, LEMON CURD
and clotted cream trifle

It may be a touch old-fashioned, but read the recipe before you start scoffing. This really is *the* English dessert, conjuring up images of children's parties during the summer months, though the Italians also have their own version of it in *zuppa inglese*. My mum, and I dare say many others, used to put together her own concoction using sponge, lots of sherry, summer fruit, jelly, custard and cream. At our house, it was always decorated with nuts and chocolate, but some friends preferred to have it with hundreds and thousands. But we don't live in the 70s any longer, so here's a quick, modern interpretation of the classic dish. It might seem strange to use Greek yoghurt, but it helps curb what can be an overly sweet dish. The decision to use Madeira cake, as well as shortbread fingers, results in a lovely contrast between the sponge-type cake and the crunchiness of the shortbread. **RS**

INGREDIENTS

250g raspberry sauce (see Extra Thyme)
250g raspberries
1 batch lemon curd
2 tbsp Greek yoghurt
200g pot clotted cream
1 bought Madeira cake
100g toasted flaked almonds
1 batch shortbread fingers

METHOD

1. Toss the raspberries together with the raspberry sauce.
2. Mix the lemon curd together with the Greek yoghurt.
3. Slice the Madeira cake thickly, and cut into rounds to the size of your chosen glass.

ASSEMBLY

1. Place a spoonful of raspberry mixture in the bottom of each glass.
2. Top with a disc of Madeira cake, then add, in sequence, a generous spoonful of lemon curd mix, another spoonful of raspberry mix, and the clotted cream.
3. Refrigerate for around 2 hours.
4. Sprinkle with the toasted almonds, and serve with 2 shortbread fingers.

CHEF'S TIPS

This trifle is only as good as the sauce that lies within it. To make the raspberry sauce, liquidise 250g of raspberries, add icing sugar and lemon to taste, then pass through a sieve. Though it may be sorely tempting, try not to indulge by dipping your spoon into the bowl at this stage! For a slightly different take on the recipe, try using variations like amaretto and mascarpone along with peaches, using the mascarpone instead of cream. Alternatively, you could use strawberries and orange curd, or bananas with cooked condensed milk – all these combinations will create trifles to die for. **AC**

RECOMMENDED WINES

8 9

Orange Muscat Essencia

THYME AFTER THYME

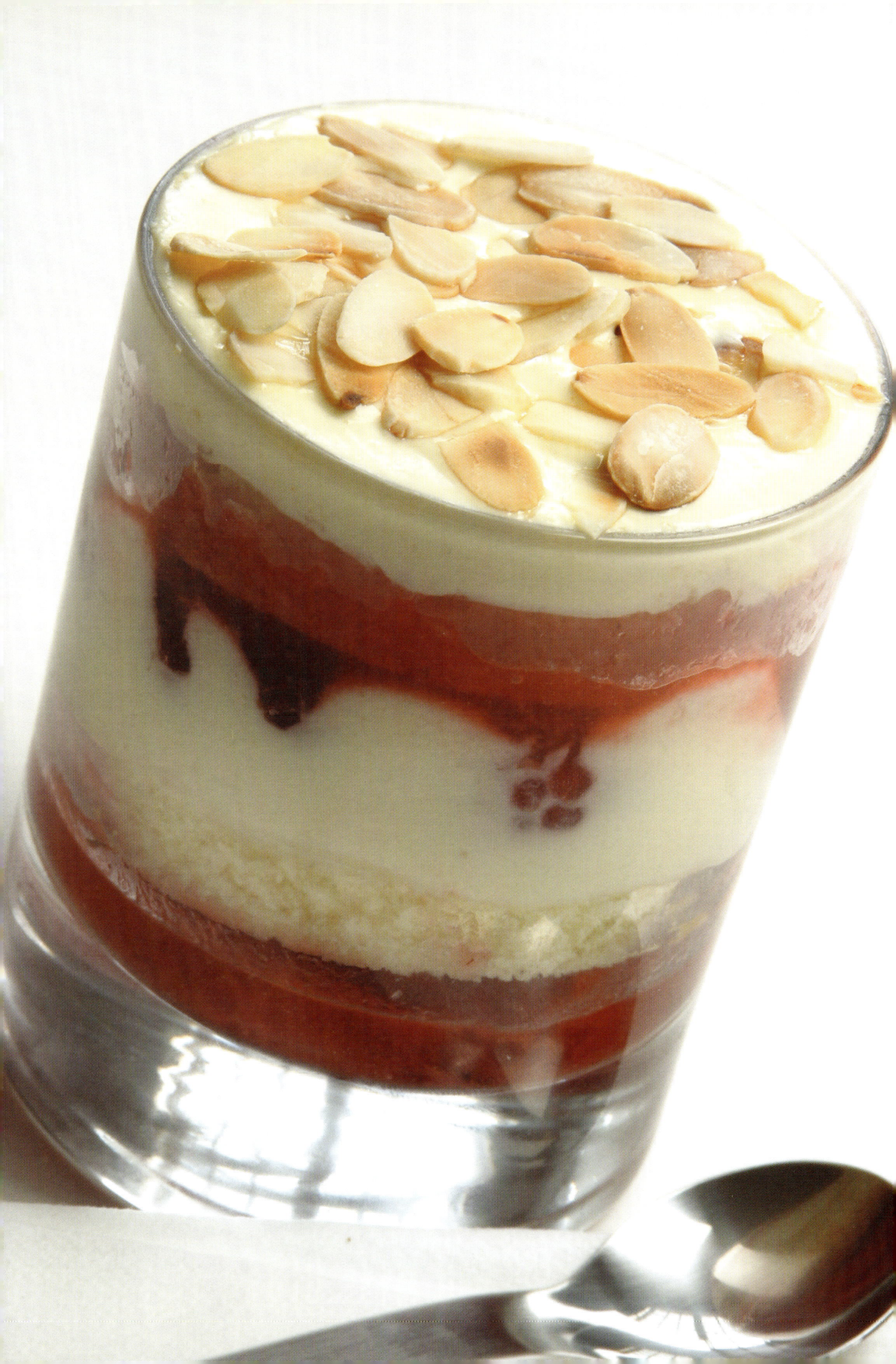

DESSERTS

RHUBARB SPRING ROLLS
with liquorice dipping sauce

We have a love affair with rhubarb in Yorkshire, and it's something I've always looked to reflect in the kitchen. I must have used rhubarb in everything over the years: brulées, fools, strudels – you name it, it's had rhubarb in it. This dish came into being during one of our periodic brainstorming sessions involving a number of chefs. Spring rolls had been under discussion earlier as a starter, and the idea transferred neatly over to the dessert menu. We've tried these flavours, and they really do work. In fact, liquorice is a natural partner for rhubarb. Going back to the Yorkshire theme, Pontefract cakes come from the town of the same name, which happens to be at the centre of the so-called 'rhubarb triangle'. **RS**

INGREDIENTS
100g butter
500g rhubarb, peeled and cut into batons
200g caster sugar
30g fresh ginger, grated
Juice of 1 lemon
100ml water
8 large spring roll wrappers
1 egg
1 batch liquorice dipping sauce (see Extra Thyme)

METHOD
1. Peel the rhubarb, and cut into batons.
2. Melt the butter in the pan, and sweat the rhubarb and ginger without colour.
3. Add the sugar, lemon juice and water, and cook until the rhubarb is softened (this should take between 5-10 minutes).
4. Pour the mix into a sieve, with a bowl underneath to collect the juice – this will be the base of the liquorice sauce. Cool down the rhubarb and keep chilled until you are rolling the spring rolls.
5. Lay out the spring roll wrappers, and place 2 tablespoons of the filling on top, about a quarter of the way up.
6. Apply an egg wash to the outside of the wrapper using a pastry brush.
7. Fold the left and right hand sides in, and roll tightly so the filling is completely enclosed.
8. Place in a pre-heated fryer at 190°c and fry until golden.
9. Drain on kitchen paper, sprinkle with caster sugar and serve with the liquorice dipping sauce.

TO SERVE
Place the spring rolls on the plate and put the liquorice dipping sauce into a small oriental dipping pot. Serve with a ball of ice-cream if desired

CHEF'S TIPS
Seasonal cooking really makes sense, especially with regards to rhubarb. It's not really suitable for cooking any time before February or March, when the excellent Yorkshire forced rhubarb becomes available. This isn't a particularly challenging dish in terms of skill, but if you are struggling with making the spring roll shape, try a beggar's purse or wan ton – as long as it looks good, it really doesn't matter. Roll the spring rolls very tightly, and avoid the air bubbles that can oil can leak inside, creating a nasty, greasy texture within. If you're really struggling with things, use two wrappers together. **AC**

RECOMMENDED WINES

8

Ch Filhot, Sauternes

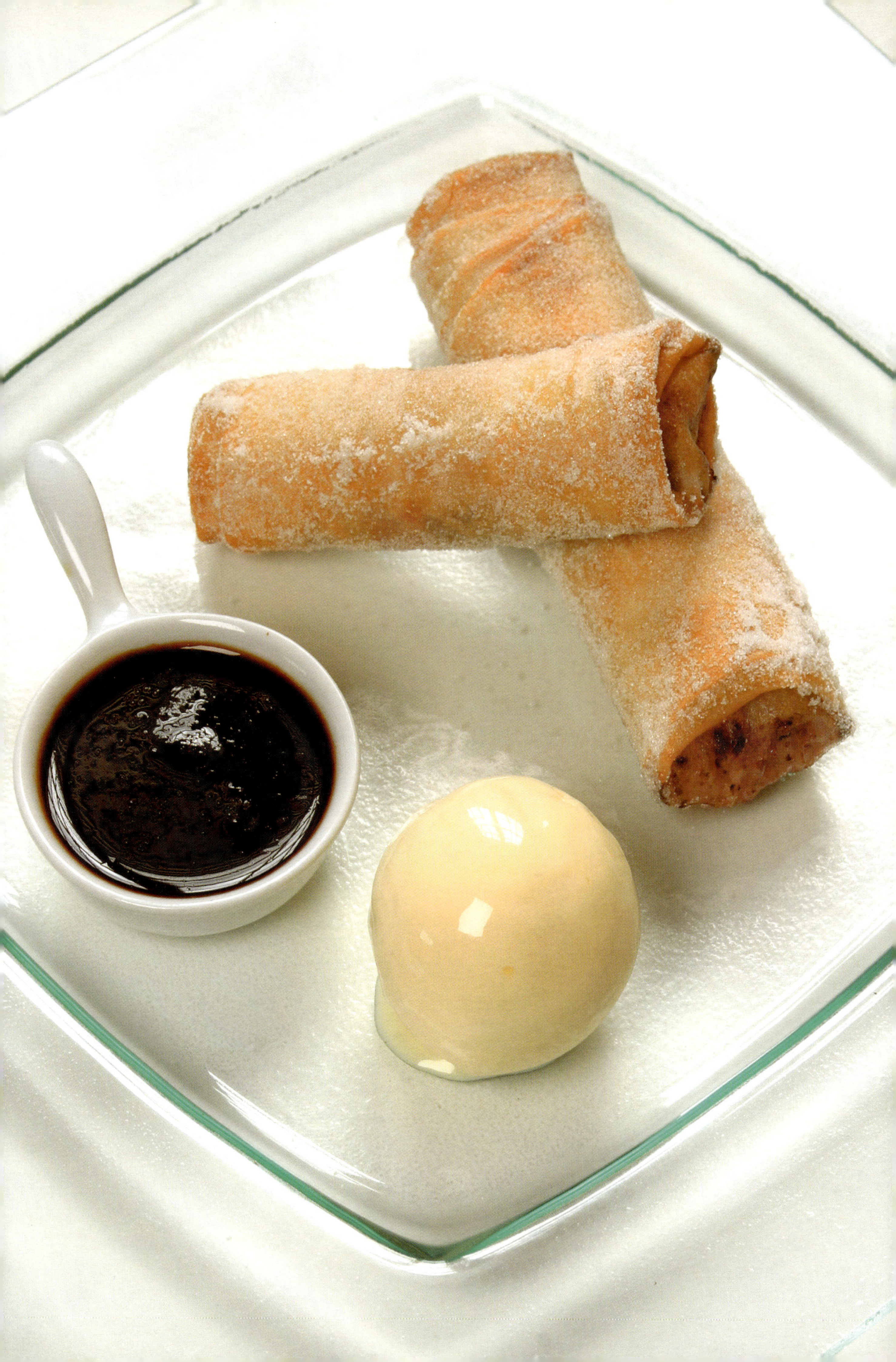

DESSERTS

CRÈME BRULÉE

This one certainly takes me back. Trio of crème brulée was on the menu the evening I opened my first restaurant, and since then I suppose you could say it has become something of a signature dish. In the years that have passed since those heady days, we must have cooked virtually every brulée under the sun. Not because they're quick and easy to make; on the contrary, this dish in particular is a very good test of a kitchen's abilities. A good crème brulée is an elusive beast indeed. Which is all the more credit to a solicitor friend of mine, whom I taught to cook a trio of crème brulée in one day on his way to the finals of television's Masterchef competition. As I've already indicated, the dish is immensely adaptable. You can add spices, chocolate, nuts and fruit. But if I was forced to narrow it down to three additional extras, I'd go for vanilla, pistachio and chocolate. **RS**

INGREDIENTS

500ml double cream
125g caster sugar
8 egg yolks
1 split vanilla pod
caster or icing sugar to glaze

METHOD

1. Whisk together the egg yolks and sugar.
2. Put the cream into a saucepan, and add the split vanilla pod (with the seeds scraped out).
3. Bring to the boil, pour over the egg yolk mixture and whisk.
4. In a clean stainless steel sauté pan, whisk the cream and egg mixture over a medium heat until it begins to bubble.
5. At this point, you should have a thick custard.
6. Make sure to whisk the mixture constantly, as it will curdle straight away if you don't.
7. Pass the cooked mixture through a sieve into a measuring jug and pour into the ramekins.
8. Set in the fridge for between 3-5 hours.
9. Before serving, sprinkle with sugar and glaze with a blowtorch, until the puddings are caramelised evenly. If you prefer a light, crisp topping, use icing sugar, but if you prefer a heavier, thicker topping, opt for caster sugar.

CHEF'S TIPS

As with so many things in life, consistency is key here. In an ideal world, it should just drop invitingly off the spoon when you are eating it. It's a difficult dish to get right straight away, but there are a few things to look out for. Firstly, the great danger with any brulée is in overcooking. Scrambled eggs do not a great dessert maketh. When the pan is on the heat, really keep that whisk going right into the corners of the pan, in order to avoid the mixture sticking. And finally, don't be afraid of using a blowtorch to give a satisfyingly darkened glaze to the topping. The more sugar you use, the more intensive caramel flavour you will get; use enough, and you'll be able to indulge in the glorious treat of cracking the top of the brulée with the back of a spoon. **RS**

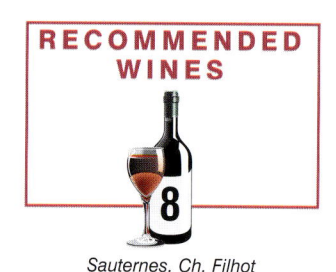

RECOMMENDED WINES

Sauternes, Ch. Filhot

THYME AFTER THYME

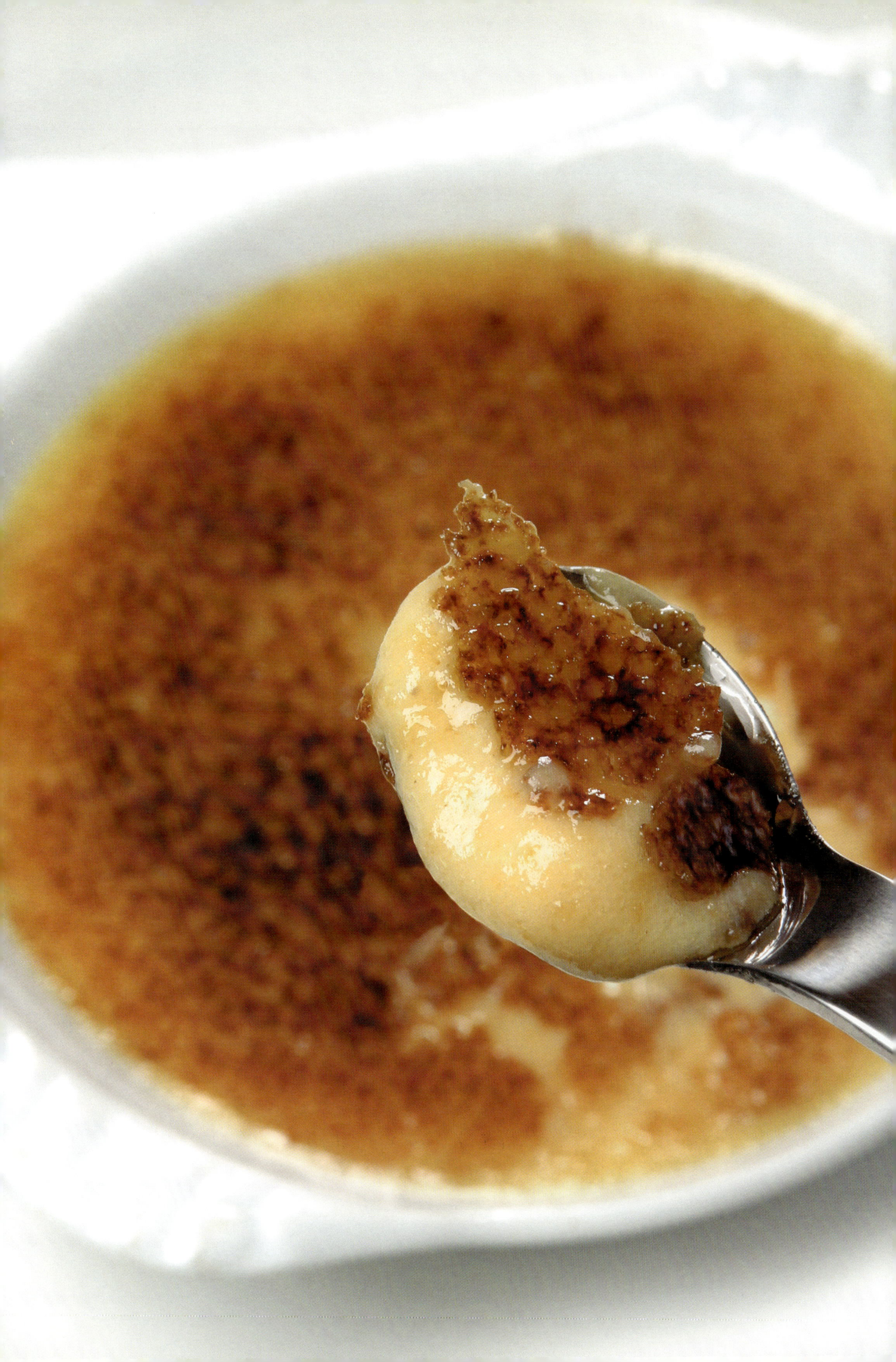

DESSERTS

FRESH BERRY PAVLOVA
with Crème Chantilly

Granted, even the merest mention of pavlova may conjure up mental images of dotty Australian housewives, but, Dame Edna jokes aside, it's a classic dessert. Made well – alas, it often isn't – the crispness of the outside contrasts beautifully with the marshmallow texture of the centre, and one serving never seems to be enough. When preparing, the supreme test of whether the meringue mixture is ready is to go in the oven is to turn the bowl upside down over your head, believe it or not. But beware. A few chefs have attempted this trick unsuccessfully, and things can quickly get messy! **AC**

INGREDIENTS

6 egg whites
160g caster sugar
300ml double cream
1 scraped vanilla pod
50g sieved icing sugar
500g mixed fresh berries
    (raspberries, strawberries,
    blueberries, redcurrants,
    blackberries)

METHOD

1 Whisk the egg whites to soft peaks.
2 Add the caster sugar and whisk until firm peaks appear.
3 With 2 large kitchen spoons, shape the mix into large quenelle-type shapes and place onto a large baking sheet lined with non-stick paper. If you wish you can pile the mix into mounds, which gives a more rustic finish to the pavlova.
4 Bake in oven at 150°c for 1 hour 15 minutes until the outside is firm but not browned.
5 Remove from oven and place on a wire rack.
6 Allow to cool before using.
7 To make the crème Chantilly, scrape the vanilla pod into the cream and add the sieved icing sugar.
8 Whip the mix to soft peaks.
9 Halve the strawberries and cut the redcurrants into small bunches.

TO SERVE

1 Place the pavlova in the middle of the plate.
2 Top generously with the crème chantilly.
3 Arrange the mixed berries over and around the pavlova .
4 Dust with icing sugar and serve .
5 This goes really well with raspberry sauce if you want to go the whole hog.

CHEF'S TIPS

Before you start anything, you need to ensure your mixing bowl is scraped clean to within an inch of its life. To do this, cut a lemon in half and go around the inside of the bowl with it; the lemon will get rid of any little specks of dirt. Don't fall into the trap of rushing out to the nearest supermarket to get hold of fresh eggs – use those that are a few days older than the very freshest and you'll end up with a fluffier result. Getting the maximum air into the egg whites is vital here, so get hold of a good machine to do the hard work for you. Hand whisking will just result in an inferior result and a very sore wrist.

If you like one berry in particular just use your preferred choice – ours are merely suggestions. But for my money there is nothing finer than English strawberries when in season. **RS**

RECOMMENDED WINES

Essencia Orange Muscat

94   THYME AFTER THYME

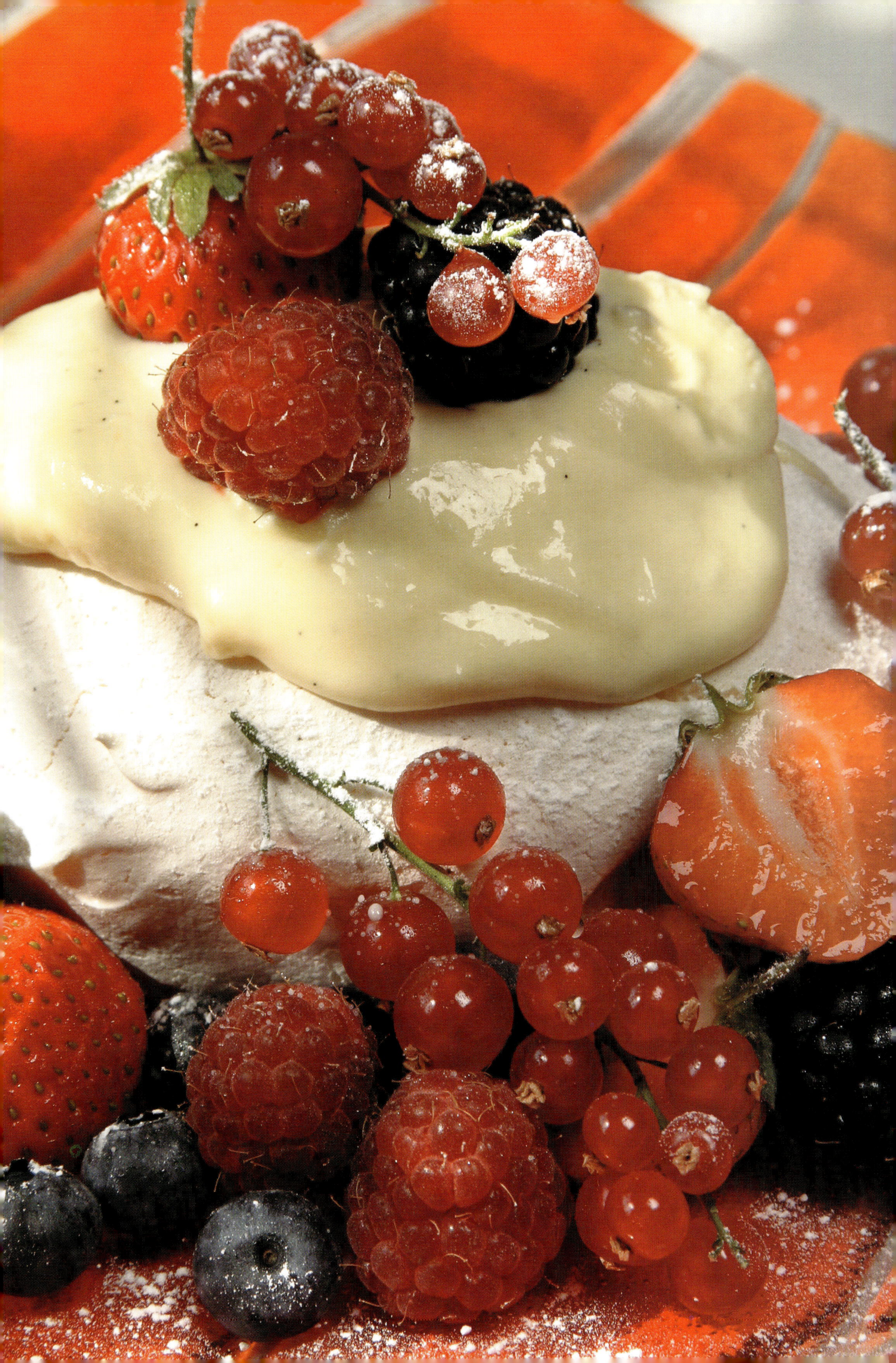

DESSERTS

CLASSIC RICE PUDDING

Ah, the memories of mum's rice pudding. I can almost smell it now, that classic, rich aroma hinting at an anticipated sweet, creamy delight. The version below is more or less the dish she served up back then, only given a little twist with the help of vanilla, cinnamon and orange peel. I've found it to be a really popular dessert in the restaurant, and it's something you can team with home-made jam, rhubarb compote, mango, caramelised bananas, or any number of other delicious toppings. You can even take it a stage further than this. At one restaurant I worked at, we used to serve rice pudding with Armagnac Agen prunes and Armagnac ice cream. It's a dish that can be used for fine dining, or as a nursery pudding, according to taste. We may not have the same food culture in the UK as, say, they do in France, but we do have a good number of staples – and this is certainly one of them. **RS**

INGREDIENTS

275ml milk
275ml double cream
60g pudding rice
25g butter
75g sugar
Small pinch of salt
1 split vanilla pod
1 cinnamon stick
1 piece orange peel

METHOD

1. Pre-heat oven to 170°c.
2. Rinse the rice in a sieve.
3. Place the cream, milk, butter, sugar, salt, scraped vanilla pod and seeds, cinnamon stick and piece of orange peel in a saucepan and bring to the boil.
4. Add the rice and re-boil.
5. Pour into an ovenproof dish, cover with tin foil and place into the oven for 1 hour.
6. Check the consistency, as you may need to add a little more cream.

TO SERVE

Spoon into ramekins, either hot or cold. This eats well on its own, but a whole diced fresh mango dressed in lime juice and spooned on top cuts through the creaminess.

CHEF'S TIPS

You've got to keep a close eye on this one. While it's important to give it enough time in the oven, there's also the danger that it will lose some of its moisture should you over-cook. Just as you would with a risotto, keep checking it every few minutes, to make sure that there is plenty of liquid left in the dish – whatever you do, don't be tempted to turn up the heat in the oven to push it along. But before you even get to the cooking stage, a word on the rice. It may be a chore, but you really must rinse it in a sieve before cooking. This process removes the starch, which tends to produce a heavy, undesirable taste. **RS**

RECOMMENDED WINES

*Mt Horrocks Cordon Cut Riesling/
Cloudy Bay Botrysized Riesling*

THYME AFTER THYME

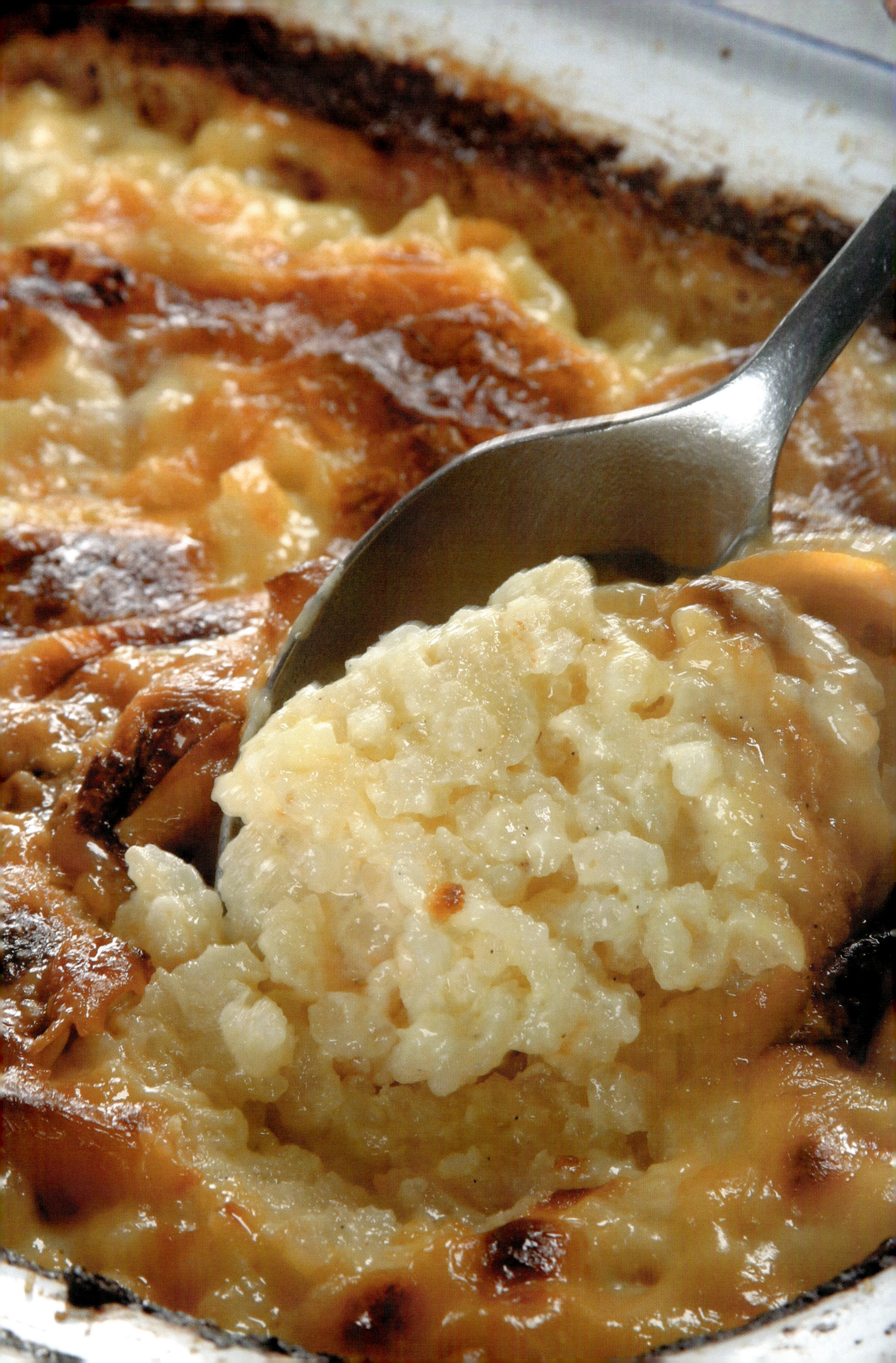

DESSERTS

VALRHONA CHOCOLATE POTS

This is a take on the classic French *petits pots au chocolat*. The result is lighter even than a crème brulée. For a pudding so indulgent, the great thing is that it's very simple to make; if you're hosting a dinner party, they can be prepared well in advance. It's a dish I cook a lot, not only for the restaurant, but also because I have a chocoholic in the family – namely, my wife Vicky. As one of life's truest pleasures. Every dessert menu has to include at least one chocolate dish, and not many have the beating of this. **RS**

INGREDIENTS

250g grated dark Valrhona chocolate
200ml milk
300ml whipping cream
6 egg yolks
100g sugar
Cocoa powder for dusting
200g creme fraiche

METHOD

1. Grate the chocolate into a stainless steel bowl, and set aside.
2. Whisk the egg yolks and sugar together in a bowl.
3. Heat the milk, bring to the boil and pour over the egg mixture, whisking well.
4. Return the mixture to a clean stainless steel saucepan and cook gently over a low to medium heat, stirring constantly with a wooden spoon (be careful at this stage, as if you don't stir constantly, or if the heat is too high, you'll end up with scrambled eggs).
5. When the mixture coats the back of a spoon, it's ready.
6. Pass it through a sieve on to the grated chocolate and whisk together well until the chocolate is melted.
7. Pour into glasses or ramekins, and chill for a couple of hours.

TO SERVE

Immediately before serving top with creme fraiche and dust with cocoa powder. Shortbread fingers accompany this dish really well.

CHEF'S TIPS

There really isn't much to say about this one, as it's pretty self-explanatory. Beware the scrambled eggs trap by carefully controlling the heat, keeping your eye on it just as you would a crème brulée. Oh, and don't eat too many in one sitting, no matter how tempting it may be – it's very rich, so too much can be tough on the stomach. **AC**

RECOMMENDED WINES

Elysium Black Muscat/Tokaji

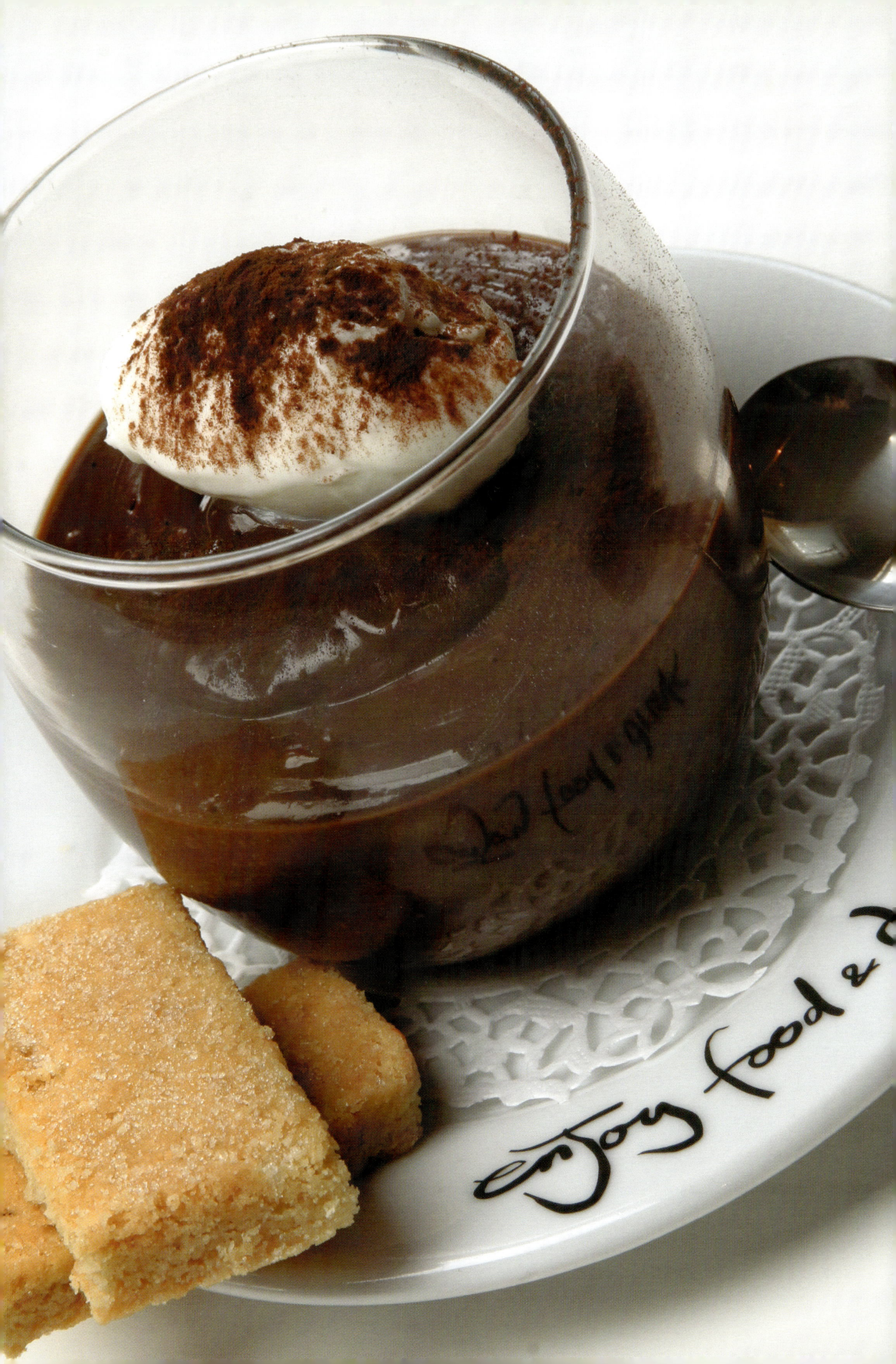
enjoy food &

DESSERTS

YORKSHIRE RAREBIT

O n the surface, it may seem strange that this is in the dessert section. But it's only like having a cheese course – and you've got to bear in mind that not everyone enjoys sweet puddings. This is a throwback to the days when a savoury was offered after dessert. It's a good staple; this recipe differs from some others in that it doesn't include sage and onion. I'd include those two for a lunch dish, but without them you don't get the heavy flavours that would weigh it down as a dessert. If you want to adapt it as a full-blown lunch dish, and want to get a little more intricate along these lines, pop it on top of a smoked haddock or beef fillet and bake it in the oven. **AC**

INGREDIENTS
400g grated Wensleydale chese
100ml milk
50g plain flour
1 whole egg
1 egg yolk
3 tsp English mustard
1 dessert spoon Henderson's Relish
1 un-sliced crusty loaf of bread

METHOD
1. In a saucepan, slowly melt the cheese and milk.
2. Add the mustard and Henderson's Relish.
3. When the cheese has melted, stir in the flour and cook out for a couple of minutes, until the mixture just leaves the sides of the pan.
4. At this stage, pour onto a tray to cool.
5. When the mix is cool enough, stir in the egg and egg yolk, and chill the mix.

TO SERVE
Lightly toast thick slices of bread on each side. Top with the rarebit, and grill until well browned.

CHEF'S TIPS
Fundamentally, it's pretty tricky to get cheese on toast wrong. Even students don't seem to have much trouble with that! But whenever cheese and milk are involved, so is a lot of fat, and the sauce can split if you're not careful in stirring and regulating the heat. Don't let the finished result cool down. Serve it bubbling away for the maximum visual effect. **RS**

RECOMMENDED WINES

CasaLapostelle Chilean Chardonnay

100 THYME AFTER THYME

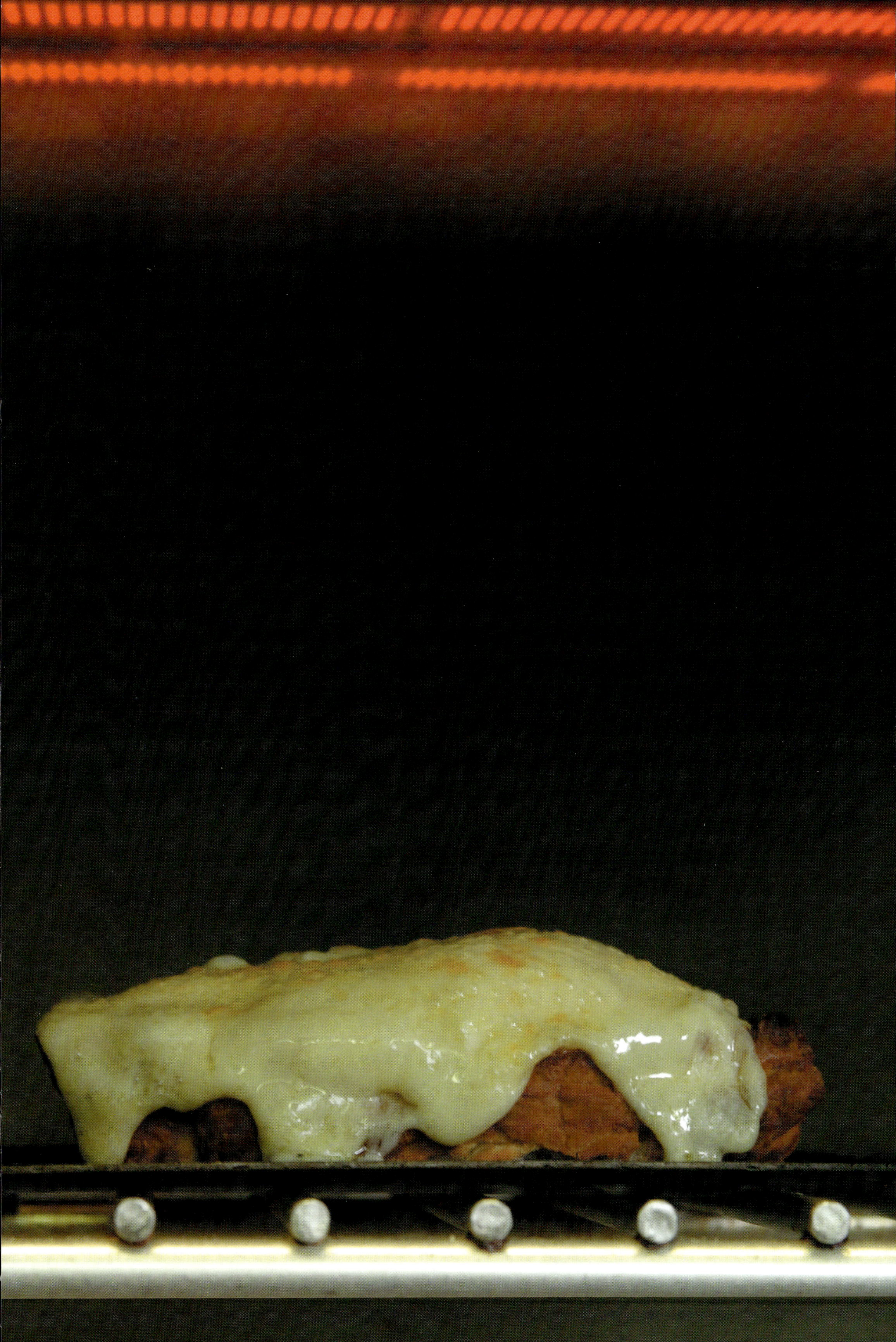

DESSERTS

RASPBERRY JELLY
with rosewater ice cream

There's a story about this one. As even those of you who aren't that familiar with Sheffield will know, we're pretty good at making things out of metal here. Although the city has always been a byword for good quality cutlery, our repertoire has extended somewhat and it's now also home to some highly-talented designers. We were asked to provide the food and drink for the tenth anniversary of one such company, and to mark the occasion, they produced a quite stunning jelly mould in pewter. This is what we made using that mould. All right, it's basically jelly and ice cream. But when some creative cookery skills meet design know-how, here's the result. If you want a dessert to make your guests' eyes pop when you bring it to the table, here it is. **RS**

INGREDIENTS

Jelly
250g raspberries
200g caster sugar
275ml water
4 leaves gelatine (soaked in cold water)

Rosewater ice cream
200g sugar
8 egg yolks
500ml milk
500ml double cream
1 tsp vanilla essence
rosewater to taste

Raspberry Sauce
To serve (see Extra Thyme)

METHOD

For the Jelly
1. Boil the sugar and water together.
2. Add the raspberries and puree in a food processor. Pass through a sieve.
3. Take a little of the raspberry mix and add the soaked gelatine.
4. Warm gently in a pan until the gelatine has melted.
5. Add to the rest of the raspberry mix and stir well so the gelatine is evenly distributed.
6. Pour into the jelly moulds and refrigerate overnight.

For the Ice Cream
1. Mix the milk, cream and vanilla in a pan. Bring to the boil.
2. Mix together the sugar and egg yolks.
3. Pour the hot milk mixture over the eggs and mix well.
4. Return the pan to a low heat and stir until the mix is nice and thick and coats the back of a spoon.
5. Pass through a sieve, place in a bowl and leave to go cold.
6. Churn in the ice cream machine if you have one or alternatively place in the freezer, stirring every 10–15 minutes until frozen.

TO SERVE
1. Turn out the set jelly into the middle of the plate.
2. Place equal quantities of strawberries and raspberries around the jelly.
3. Dust gently with icing sugar and drizzle raspberry sauce around the edge of the plate
4. Scoop a ball of ice cream and place at the side of the jelly with a shortbread biscuit.
5. Garnish with a sprig of mint and serve.

CHEF'S TIPS

Making ice cream is as easy as making custard. Invest in an ice cream machine to make the job far easier – they cost next to nothing these days. Use any mould that takes your fancy (but perhaps draw the line at the rabbit variety we all knew in childhood). And don't take fright at the presentation. Just take your time and assemble the dish immediately before serving. If your guests wonder why you've disappeared into the kitchen for a few minutes, they'll feel it was worth the wait when you reappear bearing this. **AC**

RECOMMENDED WINES
1
9

THYME AFTER THYME

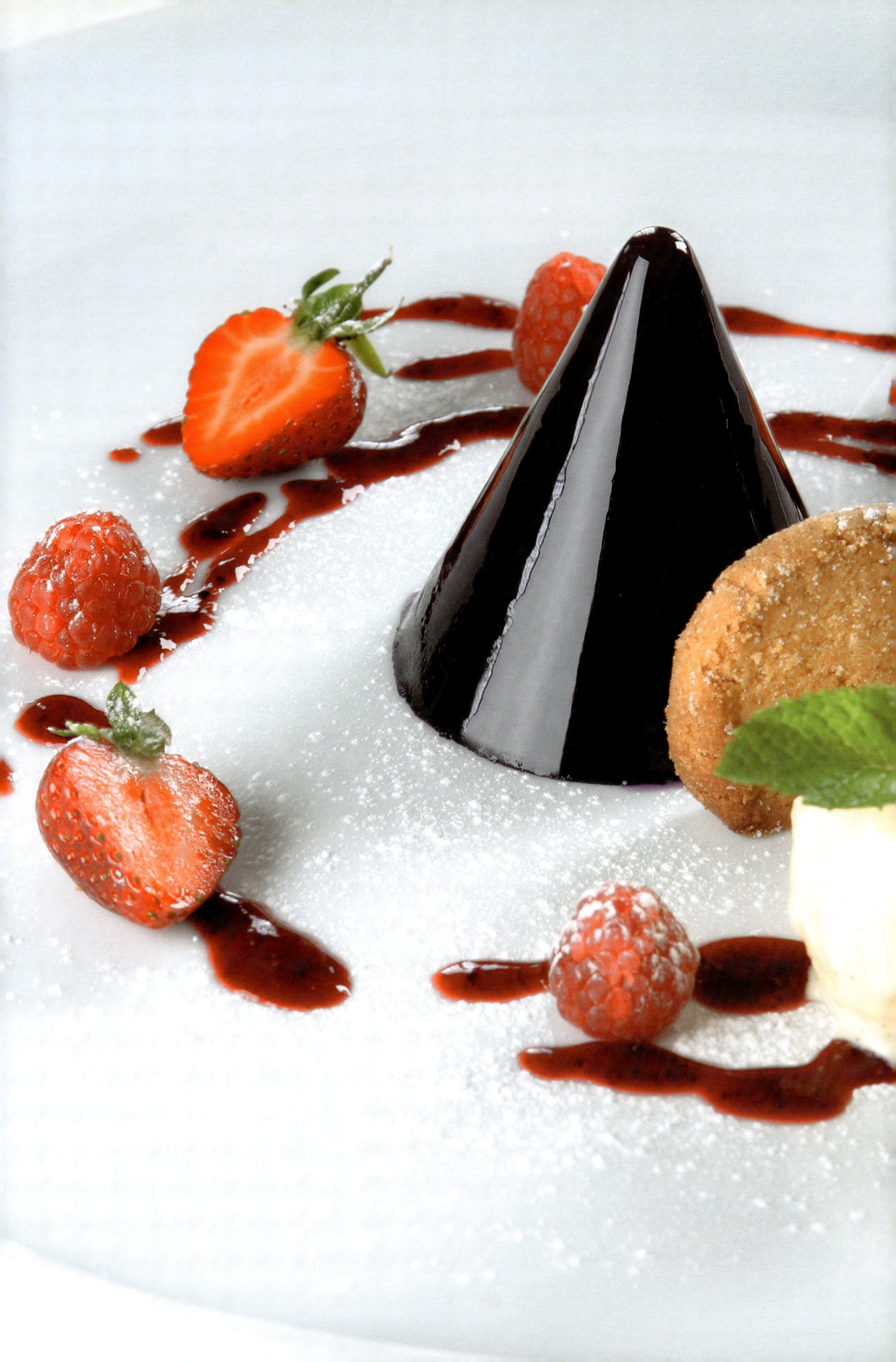

CHAPTER 5
EXTRA THYME

BASICS

MAYONNAISE

2 egg yolks
1 tsp English mustard
Pinch salt
300ml vegetable oil
1 tbsp white wine vinegar

METHOD
1. In a bowl, whisk the egg yolks together with the mustard and salt.
2. When they are well mixed together add the vegetable oil a little at a time. Keep whisking constantly until the mayonnaise becomes thick.
3. Whisk in the vinegar and taste. Add a little more salt and vinegar if required.

SALSA VERDE

65g chopped flat parsley
60g chopped coriander
20g mint
1 chopped green chilli
350g light olive oil
80g chopped capers
20g chopped garlic

METHOD
Whizz together all ingredients in blender, adding the oil steadily as the mixture combines.

SALTED ALMONDS

250g whole skin-on almonds
Maldon sea salt
Olive oil

METHOD
1. Blanch the almonds in boiling water for 1 minute.
2. Refresh in running cold water. Drain and remove skins. Place on kitchen paper to dry for a couple of hours.
3. Pre-heat oven to 180°c.
5. Place the almonds on a baking tray.
6. Pour over a little olive oil and bake for approx 5 mins. The almonds should be lightly browned.
7. Remove from oven, cool slightly, sprinkle with plenty of sea salt and serve.

TARTARE SAUCE

400g mayonnaise
Juice of 2 lemons
20g chopped flat leaf parsley
6g chopped tarragon
40g chopped capers
70g chopped gherkins
Salt
Pepper

METHOD
Combine all ingredients in a bowl. Store in an airtight container in the fridge.

AIOLI

250g mayonnaise
1 large bulb garlic
1 sprig of thyme
1 dessertspoon olive oil

METHOD
1. Separate the garlic bulb into individual cloves.
2. Place on a sheet of kitchen foil, sprinkle with olive oil and place the thyme on top.
3. Wrap into a small parcel and bake in the oven at 170°c for 40 mins–1 hour. The garlic should be soft and squeeze easily from the skin.
4. Pop each garlic clove out of its skin and mash with a fork.
5. Mix together with the mayonnaise. The aioli is now ready to serve.

PEANUT PESTO

500g unsalted peanuts (or cashew nuts)
700g good quality sweet chilli sauce
1 stick lemon grass finely chopped
4 lime leaves chopped
10g black sesame seeds
50g chopped fresh coriander (stalks as well)
10g chopped mint leaves
20g thai fish sauce
20g pickled ginger chopped
3 large cloves of garlic chopped
50g coconut cream

METHOD
Place all ingredients in food processor and blitz until nicely mixed together, don't mix for too long as the pesto will be too fine and we are aiming for a nice crunchy coarse paste.

SOY–MIRIN DRESSING

100g japanese soy sauce
100g lemon juice
100g mirin

METHOD
Combine all ingredients.

MARIE ROSE SAUCE

250g mayonnaise
2 tbsp tomato ketchup
1 tsp lemon juice
1 tsp worcestershire sauce
1 dash tabasco sauce

METHOD
In a bowl, mix all ingredients together. Keep in fridge until ready to use.

AUBERGINE DIP
(baba ganoush)

3 large aubergines
Salt
Pepper
1 tsp ground cumin
1 finely-chopped red chilli
Juice of 1 lemon
15g chopped fresh coriander
3 large cloves of garlic, finely chopped
50ml olive oil

METHOD
1. Pierce the aubergines a few times with a fork. Place on a roasting tray and cook for 1–1½ hours on 180ºc. The aubergines should be quite black when they come out.
2. Cut the roasted aubergines in half lengthways. Scoop out the flesh, chop roughly and mix with all the other ingredients.

SWEET POTATO TEMPURA

1 large sweet potato
Flour for dusting
125g plain flour
250ml sparkling water, chilled

METHOD
1. Thinly slice the sweet potato down a mandolin. Lightly dust with flour, patting off any excess.
2. Pre-heat the deep fryer to 190ºc.
3. Combine the flour with the chilled sparkling water and whisk .
4. Dip in the floured sweet potatoes and fry a few at a time until they are tender. When ready, place on kitchen paper to drain any excess oil. Lightly season with salt and serve straight away.
- If you don't have a deep fryer a wok works really well. Just half fill it with vegetable oil and heat up to medium/high heat and fry as above.
- There are also some excellent tempura batter mixes available in supermarkets. Just follow the packet instructions and you will get good results.

VIETNAMESE DIPPING SAUCE
(Nuoac Cham)

25ml thai fish sauce
½ finely diced chopped red chilli
Juice of 2 limes
15g sugar
1 crushed clove garlic
75ml water
10g chopped fresh coriander
5g chopped mint

METHOD
Mix all ingredients together and serve. This sauce should be used on the day you make it as it will discolour if kept.

CHOCOLATE ORANGE SAUCE

200g dark chocolate
50g unsalted butter
A little water
50g orange juice
grated zest of one orange

METHOD
1. Grate chocolate into a bowl.
2. Sit over a pan of simmering water and melt gently.
3. Stir in butter, orange zest, juice and water.
4. Serve

CUCUMBER & CORIANDER RAITA

350g greek yoghurt
½ diced cucumber (seeds removed)
15g chopped fresh coriander
Juice of 2 limes
Salt and pepper

METHOD
1. Remove seeds from the cucumber & cut into a medium sized dice
2. Mix together with the yoghurt, coriander, lime juice salt & pepper.

COURGETTES AND PEPPERS

2 courgettes
3 red peppers
4 large cloves garlic, crushed
Salt
Pepper
6 sprigs thyme
75ml sherry vinegar
200ml olive oil

METHOD
1. Cut the courgettes into chunky rounds. cut the peppers in half, remove the seeds and white.
2. Cut each pepper into 6 chunky pieces.
3. Pre-heat oven to 180ºc.
4. Toss the vegetables together with the thyme, olive oil, salt , pepper and garlic. place in a roasting tray and cook for approx 20–30 mins until the vegetables are nicely browned.
5. when they are out of the oven, pour over the sherry vinegar and toss together. Serve either hot or cold.

LIQUORICE DIPPING SAUCE

400ml rhubarb cooking liquor
400ml water
90g Pontefract cakes

METHOD
Bring all the ingredients to the boil. when the Pontefract cakes have melted, pass through a sieve. reserve until needed.

BASICS

ONION CONFIT

200g finely-diced onion
100ml vegetable oil

METHOD
In a medium-sized frying pan, cover the onions in oil and cook down slowly without any colour for approx 30 minutes.

LEMON CURD

6 lemons, zested and juiced
100g soft butter
8 eggs
200g caster sugar
10g cornflour

METHOD
Whisk all ingredients together in a stainless steel pan over a low heat until thick. Pass through a sieve.

STOCK SYRUP

300ml water
250g sugar

METHOD
1 Combine ingredients in a large pan and bring to the boil.
2 Simmer for 5 minutes until the sugar has completely dissolved. Chill and keep refrigerated until needed.

CHOCOLATE AND ORANGE SAUCE

300g grated dark chocolate
100g butter
100ml double cream
1 tbsp grand marnier
Finely grated zest of 1 orange

METHOD
1 Place the cream in a saucepan and gently bring to the boil, stir in the chocolate and butter.
2 Add the orange zest and grand marnier.
3 Serve.

RASPBERRY SAUCE

500g raspberries
100g caster sugar
Juice of 1 lemon
175ml water

METHOD
Place all ingredients in a pan and heat for 5 minutes. puree and pass through a sieve.

RUM AND RAISIN CUSTARD

100g sugar
8 egg yolks
275ml milk
275ml cream
50ml dark rum
25g plump raisins

METHOD
1 Soak the raisins in the rum overnight.
2 Mix the egg yolks and sugar together.
3 Bring the milk and cream to the boil. pour over the egg mix and whisk.
4 Return to a clean stainless steel pan and cook gently over low to medium heat, stirring constantly, until the custard coats the back of a spoon.
5 Remove from heat and pass the custard through a sieve into a jug.
6 Mix in the rum soaked raisins and serve.

BATTER

180g plain flour
90g self raising flour
220ml beer (chilled)
1 egg yolk
200ml semi skimmed milk
25ml vegetable oil
Salt and pepper

METHOD
Mix the batter ingredients together until it forms a smooth paste.

SHORTCRUST PASTRY

450 g plain flour
2 eggs
50ml water
200g diced butter
Pinch of salt

METHOD
1 Rub the butter and flour together until the mixture takes on a breadcrumb texture.
2 Whisk the eggs and mix with the water. Slowly add to the flour mixture and work together until a dough is formed. Wrap in cling film and rest for 1 hour.
3 To make a tart case; lightly flour work surface and roll out the pastry. Line a greased flan ring, leaving some excess pastry attached. This stops the pastry sinking.
4 Line the flan ring with greaseproof paper and fill with baking beans or rice. Bake blind at 200°c for 20–25 minutes. Remove the paper and baking beans, cool and trim.
- If you want to make sweet pastry add 100 g of caster sugar to the recipe.

BATTERED COURGETTES

2 courgettes

METHOD
1 Slice the courgettes at an angle in slices 2–3 cm thick.
2 Lightly flour, dip into the batter and fry at 170°c for 3–4 minutes or until they are lightly browned.
3 Drain on kitchen paper to remove any excess oil and season with salt.
4 Serve immediately.

BASICS

AUBERGINE CRUSHED POTATOES

2 aubergines
2 tbsp olive oil
1 medium chopped onion
2 crushed cloves garlic
8–10 cooked new potatoes

METHOD

1. Pierce the aubergines a few times with a fork, place on a roasting tray and cook for 1–1½ hours at 180°c.
2. Cut the aubergines in half lengthways and scoop out the flesh. Chop roughly and reserve.
3. In a sauté pan, heat the olive oil and gently fry the onion until soft without any colour. Add the crushed garlic and cook for a minute. Add the cooked new potatoes and crush with a fork. Season with salt and pepper and stir in the chopped roasted aubergine. Check for seasoning and serve.

LEMON SAUCE

100g finely chopped onion
250ml white wine
150ml double cream
100g butter
Juice of 2 lemons
Salt and pepper

METHOD

1. Place the chopped onion and white wine in a small saucepan.
2. Bring to the boil and reduce to a simmer for approx 5 minutes.
3. Add the double cream and return to the boil. Whisk in the butter.
4. Add the lemon juice, salt and pepper and serve.

LIME AND SESAME DRESSING

Juice of 2 limes
100ml grapeseed oil
30ml thai fish sauce
2 tsp black sesame seeds

METHOD

In a bowl, combine all ingredients with a whisk.

CHICKEN STOCK

2 roughly-chopped onions
2 celery sticks
2 leeks
2 large carrots
Half bulb of garlic
2 sprigs thyme
1 bay leaf
2kg chicken wings
Pinch of salt

METHOD

1. Peel, roughly cut and wash all the vegetables.
2. Add the chicken wings to a large stock pan and cover with approx 4 litres of water.
3. Bring to the boil with a pinch of salt. When it has reached boiling point reduce to a slow simmer and skim off all the impurities. Keep skimming until no more appears.
4. Add the washed vegetables and a little more water. Slowly simmer for 3–4 hours.
5. The stock should now be ready. Pass the stock through a fine strainer and cool.
6. It is better to make the stock a day in advance as you can refrigerate overnight. The fat sets on top – just peel off, leaving a flavoursome clear stock.

SHORTBREAD

250g plain flour
100g icing sugar
50g custard powder
200g butter
1 egg
Pinch of salt

METHOD

1. Sift the flour with the salt.
2. Cream butter, sugar and custard powder together in electric mixer. When completed, add the flour and egg at slow speed.
3. Work into a smooth dough. Wrap in cling film and chill for a couple of hours.
4. Roll out to approx 5mm thick on a lightly-floured surface and cut into fingers.
5. Preheat oven to 170°c.
6. Place fingers on to a greased baking tray or non-stick tray and bake for approx 20 minutes until a light golden colour.
7. As soon as they are removed from the oven place on a wire rack to cool and sprinkle with sugar

YORKSHIRE PUDDING

6 eggs
400g pasta flour 'tipo 00'
550 ml milk
Salt
Pepper
Vegetable oil

METHOD

1. Sieve the flour with the salt.
2. Whisk the eggs and add to the flour with the milk and pepper. It is best if you make the batter a day in advance but if necessary a few hours will do.
3. Pre–heat the oven to 220°c.
4. Take a 12-mould yorkshire pudding tray and pour a little oil in each mould.
5. Place in the oven until the oil is smoking.
6. Pour batter in each mould until almost full and bake for approx 25–30 minutes.

THYME AFTER THYME

SIDE DISHES

VICHY CARROTS

4 large carrots
Half a medium onion
60g butter
300ml water
Salt and pepper

METHOD
1 Peel and thickly slice the carrots. Finely dice the onion.
2 In a medium saucepan, melt the butter and sweat the onion without colour.
3 Add the carrots and cook for a few minutes. Season with salt and pepper.
4 Add the water and cook on a medium heat with a tight-fitting lid on the pan. This will help extract all the natural juices from the carrots.
5 They should take about 10 minutes to cook. Take care not to overcook as they shouldn't be too crisp .
6 If you wish, finish with a little chopped flat-leaf parsley.

BEETROOT HUMMUS

480g canned chickpeas (drained and washed)
300g cooked beetroot
Juice of 2 lemons
5 crushed cloves of garlic
8g ground cumin
6g ground coriander
250ml olive oil
Salt
Freshly ground black pepper

METHOD
1 Empty canned chickpeas into a colander. Drain and rinse under cold running water.
2 Put the chickpeas into a Blender with the cooked beetroot, salt, pepper, lemon juice, garlic, cumin, coriander and olive oil.
3 Liquidize until the mixture is nice and smooth. If you feel the hummus is too thick, just add a little more olive oil.
4 Check for seasoning and serve.

BUTTERED SPINACH

450g baby leaf spinach
75g butter
Salt and pepper

METHOD
1 Blanch the spinach in boiling salted water.
2 Refresh in cold water, drain and squeeze out excess water. You should be left with around 200g blanched spinach.
3 In a saute pan, heat the butter until nicely foaming and toss the spinach in.
4 Season with salt and pepper.
5 Drain on kitchen paper and serve immediately.

FRENCH BEANS LYONNAISE

300g fine french beans
150g confit onions (see basics)
Salt and pepper

METHOD
1 Blanch the french beans in boiling salted water.
2 In a saute pan, heat the onion confit.
3 Add the cooked french beans.
4 Season and serve.

THYME AFTER THYME

SIDE DISHES

CAFÉ KETCHUP

800g Heinz tomato ketchup
100g wholegrain mustard
80g french mustard
80g english mustard
Onion confit (see recipe in basics)

METHOD
In a large mixing bowl, combine the ketchup and mustards together with the onion confit.

PAK CHOY

6 heads pak choy
3 cloves chopped garlic
1 finely chopped red chilli
50ml vegetable oil
1 tablespoon japanese soy sauce

METHOD
1 Separate the leaves of the pak choy and shred the stalks.
2 Heat the oil in a saute pan and add the shredded stalks. Cover the pan with a lid and shake to prevent the stalks burning.
3 Add the leaves, chilli and garlic and replace the lid. Again, keep the pan moving.
4 When the pak choy has wilted down – about 1 minute – add the soy sauce.
5 Serve immediately.

CHILLI OIL

160ml light olive oil
160ml grapeseed oil
3 large crushed cloves garlic
2 red chillis, roughly chopped
6g mild chilli powder
10g paprika
40g tomato puree

METHOD
1 With the back of a cook's knife, crush the garlic, leaving the skin on. Cut the chillis in half lengthways then chop roughly.
2 Add the oil to a saucepan and heat gently. Add all the ingredients except the tomato puree and cook gently for about 10 minutes. It is important not to let the oil reach too high a temperature as it will taste burnt.
3 Stir in the tomato puree and cook for a further 5 minutes. Let the oil cool. A sediment will form on the bottom of the pan.
4 Strain through a sieve and allow the oil to settle again. It is now ready to serve.

HONEY ROAST PARSNIPS

4 large parsnips
100ml olive oil
2 dessertspoons clear honey
Salt
Pepper

METHOD
1 Peel, quarter and core the parsnips.
2 Heat the olive oil in a roasting tray.
3 Add the parsnips and toss in the hot oil until they are lightly browned.
4 Stir in the honey and coat the parsnips.
5 Place in the oven at 180°c for 25–30 minutes, stirring from time to time.

THYME AFTER THYME 111

SIDE DISHES

ROAST POTATOES

1.5 kg baking potatoes (or maris pipers)
Duck fat (or vegetable oil)
Maldon sea salt

METHOD
1. Peel the potatoes and cut in halves (or quarters if they are really large).
2. Place in a saucepan, cover with water and bring to the boil.
3. Reduce to a simmer and blanch for no longer than 5 minutes.
4. Drain into a colander. Return to the pan, cover with a lid and shake vigorously.
5. Meanwhile, heat the oil or fat in a roasting tray over the hob until smoking.
6. Add the potatoes and quickly turn a few times to brown. Sprinkle with salt and roast in the oven preheated to 180°c for approx 1 hour, turning regularly.
7. The potatoes should be a lovely golden brown and soft in the middle.

LYONNAISE POTATOES

1kg baby new potatoes
1 large onion, thinly sliced
Oil
Butter
Salt and pepper

METHOD
1. Boil new potatoes until just cooked. Cool and slice in half lengthways.
2. In a cast-iron frying pan, add vegetable oil and butter.
3. Heat until foaming then add the potatoes flat side down, cooking until nicely browned (about 5-6 mins each side). Place in a serving dish and keep warm.
4. In a large cast-iron frying pan, add a little vegetable oil and fry the onion until browned. Season with salt and pepper. Place on top of the potatoes.
5. When you are ready to serve, warm the potatoes through in the oven for 5 minutes.

MASHED POTATO

1kg cooked maris piper potatoes
150g butter
Salt
Pepper

METHOD
1. Peel the potatoes and boil in salted water until soft (allow 20-25 minutes).
2. With a potato masher, mash the potatoes together with the butter until smooth and free of lumps.
3. Season and serve immediately.

CHIPS

1 kg baking potatoes

METHOD
1. Peel the potatoes.
2. Pre-heat the deep fryer to 130°c.
3. Cut the potatoes into chunky style chips
4. Place the potatoes into the fryer and cook for about 20 mins. The potatoes should be a light brown colour and should break when you squeeze them between forefinger and thumb.
5. Remove from the fryer and place on kitchen paper.
6. Heat the fryer to 170°c.
7. Add the blanched chips to the oil and cook until nicely browned. This should take no longer than 2 minutes.
8. Drain on kitchen paper, sprinkle with salt and serve immediately.

112   THYME AFTER THYME

ROOT VEGETABLE MASH

1 batch mashed potato (see mashed potato recipe in this section)
3 large parsnips
3 large carrots
Half a swede
Salt and pepper

METHOD
1. Make one batch mashed potato.
2. Peel parsnips, carrots and swede. Cut into large chunks. Boil in salted water until soft (about 25 minutes).
3. Mash the vegetables down with a potato masher – don't worry if there are a few lumps in the vegetables. Mix with the plain mashed potato, season with salt and pepper and serve immediately.

MUSHY PEAS

250g marrowfat peas
Salt
Water
½ tsp bicarbonate of soda

METHOD
1. Cover the peas with water for at least 6 hours.
2. When they have finished soaking (they should have doubled in size), cover with water, bring to the boil and reduce heat to simmering for approx 1½–2 hours.
3. Add the salt towards the end of cooking.when the peas are soft and have start to melt down they are ready.
4. Add the bicarbonate of soda and cook for a further 5 minutes.
5. Check for seasoning and serve.

ROSEMARY & SEA SALT BREAD

800g bread flour
525ml warm water
12 tbsp olive oil
50g rock salt
50g sugar
100g fresh yeast
Freshly-snipped rosemary sprigs

METHOD
1. Dissolve the yeast in the warm water and 10 tbsp of the olive oil. Sieve the flour and add half of the rock salt.
2. Mix in the liquid until a dough is formed and knead for 5–10 minutes until it is nice and smooth. It is easier to do this in an electric mixer but if you don't have one just knead by hand.
3. Leave to prove in a warm place until the dough has doubled in size. Open out the dough and add the freshly snipped rosemary. Shape the dough and place in a 10 inch by 2 inch pizza tin. Prove the bread for a second time until it has doubled in size.
4. Preheat the oven to 200°c. Prod the dough with your fingers, sprinkle with the remaining salt and drizzle with 2 tbsp olive oil. Bake for about 20 minutes and cool on a wire rack.

SPRING VEGETABLE MASH

1 batch mashed potato (see recipe in this section)
40g butter
1 large shredded leek
100g garden peas
Half savoy cabbage, shredded
1 bunch chives, chopped
1 bunch flat leaf parsley, chopped
150ml double cream

METHOD
1. Make batch of plain mashed potato.
2. Shred the savoy cabbage, blanch in boiling salted water, refresh and drain. Cut the leek in half lengthways, wash and finely shred.
3. Melt the butter in a large saucepan, add the washed leeks and cook for 5 minutes until the leeks have softened a little. Add the cabbage and peas, stirring with a wooden spoon. When warm, add the mashed potato, stirring constantly. Add the cream, season and serve immediately.

CHAPTER 6
WINE AND FOOD

WINES

WINE WITH FOOD
a brief guide

1. SPARKLING WINES

There are basically three types of sparkling wines.

The first, and by far the best are made by the traditional method, as typified by Champagne. This is made by adding a yeast and sugar solution to an already made dry wine and thus causing a second fermentation to take place. The side-product of this fermentation is carbon dioxide, which causes the bubbles, or mousse, to appear in the wine. This method, used in Champagne, is also widely employed in Australia, New Zealand, Spain, USA and South Africa and produces wines that are yeasty, flavourful and delightful.

Examples are;
- Veuve Clicquot Yellow Label from Champagne,
- Cava from Spain
- Pelorus from New Zealand.

The second method is by the so-called 'Tank Method'. Wine is passed under vacuum from tank to tank to produce light and sparkly wines, such as Prosecco from Northern Italy and Sekt from Germany.

The third method, and by far the cheapest, is by the simple addition of CO_2. This makes cheap sparkling wines, but the fizz seldom stays in the glass or bottle for long. Most Sparklers under £4 a bottle are made by this method.

2. LIGHT WHITE WINES

Light white wines are great for aperitifs and simple fish dishes. Wines made from Sauvignon Blanc can be classed in this category and also some of the lighter wines from Italy, Spain and Portugal.

Sauvignon Blanc: The great grape of the Loire (Pouilly fume, Sancerre, Menetou Salon and Quincy are the major appellations) produces wines that are exceptionally aromatic and essentially minerally. They are fantastic complements to all seafood dishes.

Sauvignon Blanc is now also popping up throughout the New World. Great examples can be found from Australia, South Africa, and especially the Marlborough region of New Zealand - the phenomenal Cloudy Bay being perhaps the best-known from the region.

Muscadet from the Loire, good quality Albarinhos from Spain, Vinho Verde from Portugal and Frascati from Italy are also good examples of light white wines.

They are excellent additions to shellfish and light chicken dishes.

These wines are usually made to accompany the style of food served within the region, so in Muscadet the wines are perfect with the Oysters and Mussels famous with this region, and in northern Spain, the Albarino is a perfect accompaniment to the local fried seafood specialities.

THYME AFTER THYME

3. MEDIUM-BODIED WHITE WINES

This category is probably the most popular on sale in the UK, and includes those Aussie and southern French blends that make up the majority of all white wines sold today.

These blends include Semillon/Chardonnay, Sauvignon/Semillon and the Marsanne/Roussanne blends of Southern France.

These blended wines from South Australia represent fabulous value for money, great tastes, and ideal partners to light white meat dishes such as chicken and pork. The downside is that most are produced in such huge quantities that sometimes quality is let down to market forces so it maybe worth paying a couple of extra pounds to get something that offers quite a lot more flavour and varietal characteristics.

From Bordeaux and the south of France, these blended wines are usually made from Sauvignon Blanc and Semillon, a grape variety that offers body and a certain lusciousness to the finished wine, and also adds a lovely perfumed aroma to the wine.

Also from the northern Burgundy region there are some great examples of medium bodied wines from the Chablis region. Having been given a pretty bad press in the eighties and nineties, the better Chablis producers are now giving us some cracking examples of steel and minerally Chardonnay at its best. They are a fabulous accompaniment to lighter meat dishes such as rack of lamb and richer chicken and fish dishes

In Italy, medium-bodied white wines include the luscious Pinot Grigio from the north-east, steely Gavi from around lake Garda and now experimentation with international grape varieties is giving us examples of Chardonnay and Sauvignon from around the country.

Riesling is another grape variety that fits into this category. From the mountains of Alsace, and valleys of the Rhine to South Australia and New Zealand this noble variety provides a fascinating range of styles and tastes. They can range from light and flowery to thick and petrolly, from bone-dry to exceptionally sweet. This is a variety that can fit any taste or budget.

4. FULL-BODIED WHITE WINES

Most people don't see white wines as being full-bodied but a lot of oaked chardonnay wines are of this ilk. The great wines of Burgundy, such as Puligny and Chassagne Montrachet, Meursault and the single grand cru vineyard of Montrachet certainly justify the tag. These are rich, powerful wines for long aging, although some can be drunk at 2–3 years of age, depending on the producer and style of wine. These wines exhibit aromas of freshly baked brioche and croissants with lemon and lime undertones in their youth and melony rich aromas with age. They can be drunk with a host of dishes and can enhance any meal.

Also the great Chardonnays from Napa and Sonoma in California and from Oregon and Washington can also fit this bill. A number of French-influenced winemakers are now making quality wines from Chardonnay that can match most of France's finest. Unfortunately they often have prices to match.

RED WINES

Red wines come in all shapes and sizes from all over the world and often it is difficult to find the one that's just right. Maybe we have had a wine whilst on holiday which at the time was fantastic, but when at home rarely lives up to expectation. Why? On holiday we are relaxed and enjoying new things, as well as food and wine. On a beach all is well with the world, but back home on a rainy, cold evening things just aren't the same. Retsina from Greece, Sangria in Spain and Vat wine from France are prone to being bad travellers.

In most of Europe where wine is made, it is seldom drunk on its own. In Italy and Spain for example wine is only consumed with food and it is an integral part of any family meal (where large quantities of everything are consumed). Therefore these wines are probably not that good as aperitifs but are fantastic when accompanied by the right dish. Elsewhere the lighter French Reds from Beaujolais, the Loire and Languedoc are great aperitif wines and can be enjoyed in their own right.

5. LIGHTER REDS

These come from a couple of grape varieties, notably Gamay and Pinot Noir. Gamay is the great grape of Beaujolais and produces light, fruity fresh wines that are fantastic to drink on their own or as accompaniments to Antipasti, cooked and cured meats and lighter cheeses.

Pinot Noir is the great red grape of Burgundy. Those funny-sounding appellations from Nuits St Georges through Vosne Romanee and Chambertin are all made from this grape variety. These are great wines for lighter meat dishes such as lamb and veal also can be a good accompaniment for some spicy Thai dishes.

Nice Light Pinot can also be found from countries such as New Zealand, where great examples come from regions such as Marlborough, Martinborough, Otago and Hawkes Bay, and also South Africa, especially from the Vineyards around Walker Bay.

6. MEDIUM-BODIED RED WINES

This is perhaps the largest category because in here we find wines from Italy, Spain, Argentina, Chile, Australia, South Africa and New Zealand, and embrace a large number of grape varieties ranging from Tempranillo in Rioja to Sangiovese in Italy to Grenache, Merlot, Cab Franc, Petite Syrah and many More.

Italy is a book in itself but the most important wines are those from the Nebbiolo grape from the northeast and the Sangiovese Grape from Tuscany and beyond.

Nebbiolo produces the wines of Barolo and Barberesco. These wines offer flavours of ripe red cherries and are great accompaniments to italian food.

Down in Tuscany the Sangiovese grape is King. It makes the wines of Chianti, Brunello and Montepulciano. Each offers different characteristics and is great with the regional foods for which we are so familiar

Some other notable medium bodied wines come from the Grenache Grape in the south of France and the Rhone where some great wines are made in The Cotes du Rhone and Chateauneuf du Pape regions.

As for California, great Examples from Kistler and Marcassin will delight the senses but strain the wallet.

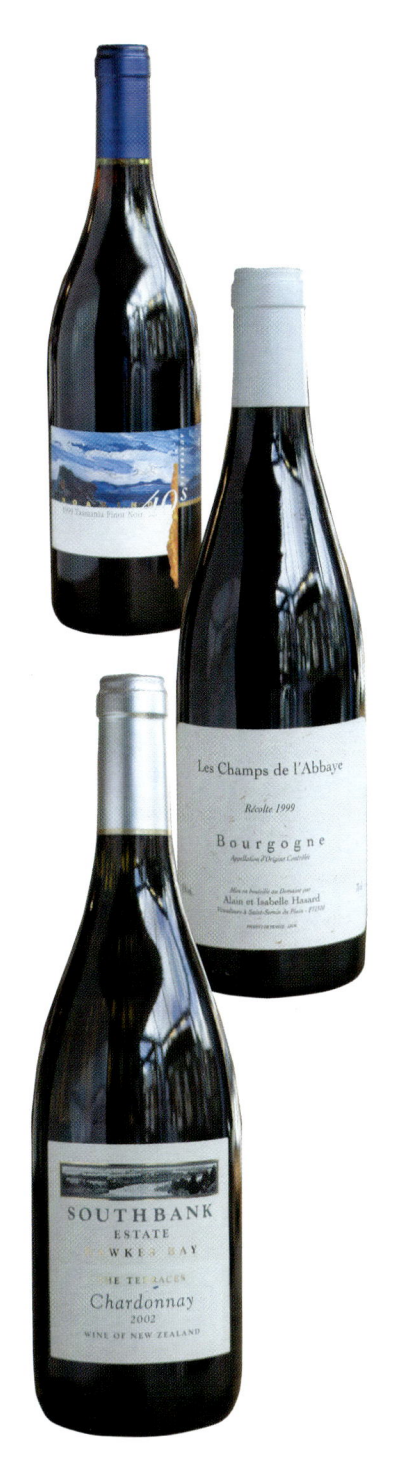

7. FULL-BODIED RED WINES

From the classic varieties of Merlot, Cabernet Sauvignon and Shiraz, these are the wines we come across most, either as single varietal in Australia and the rest of the new world or as Blends such as in the great wines of Bordeaux. These are wines with good alcohol, tannins and ripe fruit that are the great accompaniments for our red meat dishes, savoury stews, a variety of cheese and many more dishes.

Here are but a few of the better-known examples of the style;
- Bordeaux, chateau bottled – a blend of Cab S, Merlot and Cab Franc
- St Emilion – Cab Franc and Merlot
- Pomerol – Merlot and a little Cab Franc
- Barossa Shiraz
- Coonawarra Cabernet
- Heathcote Shiraz
- Hermitage
- Crozes Hermitage – Rhone Syrah
- Cote Rotie – Northern Rhone Shiraz
- Pinotage and Cabernet from S.Africa
- Chilean and Argentina Varietal
- California Cabernet and Merlot.

8. DESSERT WINES

Made from either late harvest grapes or those attacked by Botrytis (noble rot) or by drying the grapes to raisins, dessert wines are great accompaniments for not only puddings, but cheese and certain savoury dishes like foie gras.

9. FORTIFIED WINES

These are made by the addition of grape spirit (brandy) to low-alcohol, fermenting wines allowing the fermentation to stop and a sweet, unctuous wine to be formed. There are many examples around the world in many different styles, such as;
- Sherry – Spain – dry and sweet varieties
- Port – The great wine of the Douro – Vintage years can last for decades
- Madeira – from the Island of the same name
- Banyuls – South of France
- Maury – South of France
- Rutherglen Muscat and Tokay from Australia

QUICK-REFERENCE KEY TO WINE STYLES

You'll also find a general style of wine recommended on each recipe page. Each is denoted by one of the following numbers. Just see the main text in this section to find out more about each style.

1 – sparkling – dry
2 – light white
3 – medium white
4 – full white
5 – light red
6 – med red
7 – full red
8 – dessert
9 – fortified

Peter Goulding has been a photographer, shooting still life, fashion, editorial and food for many years now; in fact his first ever professional colour photograph was of food taken at Blackpool College of Art, where he studied photography. It was the college's first ever colour photograph produced on the premises also, so that's a bit of a landmark, much like this book and the photographs in it.

All the images have been shot digitally, probably another first in food photography. But, like anything which has elements of creativity in it, like the recipes from Richard and Adrian, things are not always straightforward.

"Shooting digitally allows me to take complete control of the finished image. With film it's normally passed on to a repro house who will crop and adjust the image to match it with their requirements, and not even consult the photographer how he saw the end result. Now that's all changed and it also allows me to think digitally before I begin to take shots. For instance the picture on page 37 of the scallops cooking in the pan is the result of three different images. Not that the shot's cheating in anyway – the scallops were cooked just like you see but in recording the scallops the flames just disappeared and so these had to be brought back in from another live exposure shot and married with the sharp image of the scallops. What the eye sees is not always what film or digital records, so you have to be more aware of what's missing and try to put it back."

When Peter was asked to contribute to the book using his skills as a photographer he had no hesitation in accepting the challenge. After all he had eaten before at Thyme and knew the quality of the food was top drawer and as a keen home chef himself felt he could learn a lot from this experience.

"My waistline expanded in direct proportion to the knowledge I gained from these two top chefs", he remarked "and now I have to tone it down a little perhaps concentration for the rest of the year on the wine section."

Having gained numerous awards over the years, we feel pretty confident that this book can only add to the reputation of Peter being a top creative photographer in his field.

Peter can be contacted by email at studio@Eeleven.co.uk for all photographic commissions.

INDEX

B
Baked chocolate pudding	82
Banana and banoffee crumble	84
Bang bang chicken with vegetable salad	70
Boiled ham hock with grain mustard sauce and spring vegetable mash	54
Braised lamb shanks with root vegetable mash	48
Braised Teryaki mushrooms	78
Bruschetta with fig and mozzarella	44

C
Chicken Breast with Mozzarella and Parma ham	22
Classic rice pudding	96
Crabcakes with sweetcorn chowder	56
Crème brulée	92

D
Duck and oriental vegetable spring rolls	64

F
Fish and chips	42
Fishcakes with green vegetables and butter sauce	52

H
Hot and sour soup with seafood	66

I
Italian sausages with polenta mash & tomato sauce	12

L
Linguine with garlic, lemon, chilli and rocket	32

M
Meat and potato pie	50
Mussels with garlic cream sauce	46

O
Onion tart with Manchego cheese	40

P
Pasta Genovese	18
Pavlova with crème Chantilly	94

R
Raspberry jelly with rosewater ice-cream	102
Raspberry, lemon curd and clotted cream trifle	88
Red pepper risotto	24
Rhubarb spring rolls with liquorice dipping sauce	89
Ribeye Steak with Teriyaki sauce	74
Roast beef and Yorkshire pudding	38

S
Salmon and prawn curry	68
Salmon miso with soba noodle salad	76
Seared tuna with mango–jalapeno salsa	26
Scallops with fennel remoulade	36
Shell-on prawns with dipping sauces	16
Smoked haddock gratin	14
Spaghetti Bolognese	58
Spicy Portugese pork and white bean stew	28

T
Thai prawn cakes	72
Thai-style chicken udon noodle bowl	62
Thyme Café cheeseburger	20

V
Valrhona chocolate pots	98

W
Warm cherries with Mascarpone	86
Whole roast sea bass with Lyonnaise potatoes and salsa verde	30

Y
Yorkshire rarebit	100